Praise for
INTENTIONAL TEACHING in
Early Childhood

"Offers a valuable guide to new and experienced teachers. As they read and do the exercises, early educators will be able to reflect on their practice, their goals, and their career. This book can be used individually or with a study group of colleagues meeting to share their passion for a profession that is as challenging as it is rewarding. In the end, the children will benefit from their intentional teachers."

—Angèle Sancho Passe, early childhood education consultant and author of *Evaluating and Supporting Early Childhood Teachers*

"A must read and excellent educator guide about reflection and relationships. *Intentional Teaching in Early Childhood* gives teachers multiple, concrete resources and support for how to reflect on the complexities of a teaching life. As the authors state: 'The changes are not just coming at you; they are happening inside you.'"

—Tamar Jacobson, Ph.D., author of *Don't Get So Upset! Help Young Children Manage Their Feelings by Understanding Your Own*

"A careful, complete approach to continuous development of teachers, by teachers. The book speaks directly to teachers, helping them develop and articulate goals, worries, questions, and areas of change. While it is supportive of teachers at any level, it also challenges them to continue to explore and respond, to recognize areas of conflict or complacency, and to stay in touch with other opinions. A wonderful tone, full of examples, while at the same time demanding, clear, and based on research and experience!"

—Cindy Ballenger, teacher-researcher and author of *Puzzling Moments, Teachable Moments*

"Inquiry and reflection are the key to lifelong professional growth as a teacher. They are especially powerful when integrated with organized structures for ongoing dialogue with other adults. This book offers many reasons, stories, and tools to help early childhood educators seeking to promote intentional teaching for themselves and their colleagues."

—Carolyn Pope Edwards, Cather Professor Emeritus, University of Nebraska-Lincoln

"This book aims to support teachers in driving their own professional development. Useful concepts include knowing your beliefs and values, understanding stages of teacher development and the change process, integrating new knowledge into practice, and advocating for organizational support. *Intentional Teaching in Early Childhood* is a valuable resource for developing teacher intentionality, professionalism, and leadership."

—Margie Carter, coauthor of *Training Teachers: A Harvest of Theory and Practice; The Visionary Director;* and *Learning Together with Young Children*

INTENTIONAL TEACHING in Early Childhood

Ignite Your Passion for Learning and Improve Outcomes for Young Children

Sandra Heidemann, M.S.
Beth Menninga, M.A.Ed.
Claire Chang, M.A.

Foreword by Carol Brunson Day

free spirit
PUBLISHING®

Library of Congress Cataloging-in-Publication Data
Names: Heidemann, Sandra, 1946– author. | Menninga, Beth. | Chang, Claire.
Title: Intentional teaching in early childhood : ignite your passion for learning and improve outcomes for young children / Sandra Heidemann, Beth Menninga, Claire Chang.
Description: Minneapolis : Free Spirit Publishing, 2019. | Series: The thinking teacher | Includes bibliograph-ical references and index. | Identifiers: LCCN 2018056918 (print) | LCCN 2018060024 (ebook) | ISBN 9781631984273 (Web PDF) | ISBN 9781631984280 (ePub) | ISBN 9781631984266 (paperback) | ISBN 1631984268 (paperback)
Subjects: LCSH: Early childhood education—United States. | Early childhood teachers—In-service train-ing—United States. | Early childhood teachers—Professional relationships. | Learning, Psychology of. | Teaching—Philosophy. | BISAC: EDUCATION / Professional Development. | EDUCATION / Preschool & Kindergarten.
Classification: LCC LB1139.25 (ebook) | LCC LB1139.25 .H44 2019 (print) | DDC 372.21—dc23
LC record available at https://lccn.loc.gov/2018056918.

Image credits: page 3 © Martin Malchev | Dreamstime.com; page 9 © Monkey Business Images | Dreamstime.com; page 47 © Photographerlondon | Dreamstime.com; page 74 © Guernica | Dreamstime.com; page 80 © Thiagiruiz | Dreamstime.com; pages 85–86, 154–155 © PureSolution | Dreamstime.com; page 106 © Mishkacz | Dreamstime.com; page 124 © Chantalnathalie | Dreamstime.com; pages 123–124 © Oleksandr Melnyk | Dreamstime.com; pages 127–128 © Julynx | Dreamstime.com; page 131 © Monkey Business Images | Dreamstime.com

Cover by Shannon Pourciau, Interior design by Colleen Rollins and Emily Dyer; Production by Emily Dyer
Edited by Meg Bratsch and Christine Zuchora-Walske

10 9 8 7 6 5 4 3 2 1
Printed in the United States of America

Free Spirit Publishing Inc.
6325 Sandburg Road, Suite 100
Minneapolis, MN 55427-3674
(612) 338-2068
help4kids@freespirit.com
www.freespirit.com

FSC
www.fsc.org
MIX
Paper from
responsible sources
FSC® C005010

Dedication

We want to dedicate this book to two groups of people who were instrumental in our success: the trustees of the F. R. Bigelow Foundation, who courageously championed our efforts for our community, and the teachers, coaches, children, and families who participated in our professional development initiatives. The teachers, especially, taught us way more than we were able to share with them. They inspired us, and this book is really the story of their journeys.

Acknowledgments

It is difficult to list everyone who contributed to the two projects we initiated: Words Work! and Numbers Work! First of all, we are grateful for the support of our funders: F. R. Bigelow Foundation, The Saint Paul Foundation, and Mardag Foundation. Their generosity made everything possible. We especially thank Bob Bullard and John Couchman, who were our champions and steadfast supporters. We could not have done it without you.

Our partner programs were willing and ready to engage in the process of learning together about early literacy and math. They helped us problem-solve schedules and logistics and supported their teachers as the teachers attended trainings and analyzed data. Our partner programs include the following Head Start programs: Community Action Partnership of Ramsey and Washington Counties, Heartland Community Action Agency, Mille Lacs Band of Ojibwe, Northwest Community Action, Three Rivers Community Action, West Central Minnesota Communities Action, and Community Action Partnership of Scott, Carver, and Dakota Counties; preK programs at Community of Peace Academy and Independent School District 622; and the following child care programs: Community Child Care Center (Saint Paul) and Wilder Child Development Center.

A big thanks to our evaluation team: Mary Ellen Murphy, Vanessa Stephens of Face Valu Evaluation Consulting and Associates, and Stella Zimmerman from ACET Inc. They guided us as we formed a framework for our theory of change. Debbie Hewitt helped us articulate our model. This model was invaluable as we adapted to different sites and content matter.

We couldn't have done this without the support and encouragement of our editors, Meg Bratsch and Margie Lisovskis at Free Spirit Publishing and Kara Lomen at Redleaf Press. They patiently answered our questions, offered suggestions, and gave welcome feedback. A special thanks to Christine Zuchora-Walske, who carefully went through our manuscript chapter by chapter to ensure we were saying what we wanted to say. Thank you, Free Spirit and Redleaf.

We are grateful to the National Association for the Education of Young Children (NAEYC), who exposed us to national experts in the field of early childhood education, and to Gayle Kelly of the Minnesota Head Start Association, who was a great ally as we expanded our model to Greater Minnesota. Dr. Sally Moomaw and her husband, Charlie, provided hours of technical assistance in the thoughtful application of Sally's early math assessment tool. Their charts and graphs helped us share our results with teachers and funders alike.

We thank our spouses and children for supporting, feeding, and encouraging us as we worked. We are sure they sometimes wondered how we were going to get the book done. But we did, thanks to their confidence that we could.

CONTENTS

PART 3: GETTING WHAT YOU NEED

LIST OF FIGURES

LIST OF REPRODUCIBLE PAGES

Reproducible pages can be downloaded and printed out. See page 200 for downloading instructions.

FOREWORD

by Carol Brunson Day, Ph.D., past president of the NAEYC Board and CEO of Brunson, Phillips & Day Consultants

It is an extraordinarily timely event for a newly published book in 2019 to call itself *Intentional Teaching in Early Childhood: Ignite Your Passion for Learning and Improve Outcomes for Young Children*. As evidenced just last year by the National Association for the Education of Young Children's (NAEYC) newly minted mission statement—which, for the first time since its founding in 1926, identifies advancing the profession as a core component of its work—we are at the dawn of an intentional movement in the field of early education focused on teachers.

Although a timely and exciting topic, the idea of intentionality in teaching is not new. This notion of a teacher being in full awareness of what she or he is doing, and thoughtful and mindful about teaching and learning with children and families, is a well-established ideal for what we want all teachers to be. However, how to achieve this in today's world, where the distractions of changing curriculum models and assessments abound, continues to beg for answers.

Sandra Heidemann, Beth Menninga, and Claire Chang bring their vast firsthand experience working with hundreds of teachers over fourteen years as they explore and analyze intentionality and contribute a unique perspective for today's early education scene. In their own words, they seek to "demystify how to support the full development of teachers." Sounds simple, yes? But their approach to professional development is deeply analytic and subtly unique. And it arrives at an important moment, one in which there is a seeming explosion of effort to provide early learning initiatives, mainly focused on increased content knowledge and improved interactional teaching strategies with and for children. These authors take a different approach, zeroing in on the teacher's professional development as a teacher. Though the distinction is subtle, it is clearly a shift away from the *how-tos* and the *to-dos* in the classroom with materials to the *who-am-Is* and *why-am-Is* in the teacher's role with children and others. As you read, you will come to understand and feel the shift.

As we try to learn new things, we often want specifics. But sometimes specifics become recipes that teachers feel compelled to copy or mimic. This volume manages to avoid that formula. That is, while it is full of specifics—stories from teachers and about other teachers, stories about children in classrooms, recommendations about interactions with parents—the specifics are used in ways that open up new possibilities for thinking about *how to think about* who one is as an early childhood education professional. The authors achieve this by always keeping the teacher in the active role of constructing his or her own practice. As they coach their readers through thinking, reflecting, analyzing, and struggling to understand in new ways, they always convey a sense of confidence in teachers' efficacy to achieve the desired result.

This, too, is a remarkable achievement: the way the authors exude such confidence in the power of teachers not only to participate in the transformation of their own practice but also to have an impact on the institutions in which they work. In reading this book, I was convinced that as teachers we can tackle the common and perhaps inevitable roadblocks to change (no money, too busy, too much resistance, don't think we should do that right now) without letting them overwhelm us, turning them instead into "opportunities to become more innovative thinkers and doers." In many ways, the authors place teachers in a position of power over their own professional development. They offer specific tactics, like "Think about ways you can influence those who plan your staff training," and complex strategies, like uncovering the dynamics of one's own professional growth.

Moreover, as a result of their rich professional lives, Sandra Heidemann, Beth Menninga, and Claire Chang are able to share many illustrative stories that bring their points to life. Writing simultaneously *about* teachers and *for* teachers, they have used a captivating style and format that are full of emotion and life.

So what are my favorite parts? Since I have always thought that struggling with contradicting ideas helps people think better, I love the way the text treats wrestling with dilemmas as rich opportunities to become more conscious of your values and priorities about teaching. Defining a dilemma as arising when you have to choose between two competing or contradictory ideas, the authors encourage working through challenges like feeling stuck as part of the *process* of resolution and as a *means* to it. They encourage us to accept the discomfort that comes from making mistakes and being in disequilibrium—really important for teachers to hear!

As I read, I felt a certain joy and pride as an early childhood education professional in today's world. The way in which the authors write tells so much about who they are as persons. Sensitive. Observant. Creative. Caring and committed enough toward everyone in this world to discuss culture and family engagement in meaningful ways, and to write about disenfranchised communities as models of strength. These are the kind of people we as a profession should want to tell our story. And although I know only one of the authors (Claire Chang) personally, I feel confident saying that all three represent the best that we possess as an early childhood education profession.

These authors have done a splendid and exciting job of identifying how to face the challenges that change presents. As you read their work, you will feel you're being walked through the ideas with your hand held every step of the way by someone who has been on this journey before.

Carol Brunson Day

INTRODUCTION

Your development as a teacher is important not only to you, but also to your students, their families, and your whole community. When you *want* to be the very best teacher you possibly can be, everyone benefits.

Sometimes you might feel lost, marginalized, or forgotten in the midst of quality and accountability trends. Regulations, assessments, student-teacher ratios, and environment do contribute to quality and accountability. But it's the better teachers who create better outcomes. Your ability to reach for your best grows when you're able to define for yourself how you came to teaching, what you learn from teaching, and how you can grow as a teacher while vigilantly keeping children's success as your focus.

This book provides a framework for teacher-directed professional development—regardless of your length of time in the field, your stage of teacher development, or the age of your students. It is a tool not only for you and your fellow teachers, but also for the supervisors, directors, managers, coaches, and principals who guide and inspire your work. You can use this tool to help you take control of your path as a professional committed to facilitating learning for every child.

Why Intentionality?

The word *intentional* means "made, given, or done with full awareness of what one is doing." We propose that when teachers teach with a full awareness of what they are doing, better learning is the result. Children not only have better academic outcomes, they also have better social and emotional outcomes.

We learned about the power of fostering intentionality in teaching through two distinct projects. The first project focused on how to increase literacy and kindergarten readiness in a Midwestern state among children of color, children whose families had low income, and children whose home language was not English. In the second project, we worked with children who had these characteristics to achieve early math outcomes needed for success in school and life.

In both cases, we collaborated with preschool programs in our local community, including Head Start, nonprofit preschools, nonprofit child care centers, and preK programs operated by a school district and a charter school. In both projects, children achieved statistically significant growth in reading or math. In some cases, children's gains doubled, tripled, or even quadrupled their initial scores. This occurred despite program variations in curriculum, teacher credentials, student demographics, program structure, and composition of teaching staff. People often ask us about the secret to our success.

This book unveils our secret. We found that when we invest in teachers' intentionality, teachers change. They stand taller, speak more clearly, assert their knowledge and experience, and advocate for their students. Intentional teachers use resources wisely. They share their perspective and knowledge with others. Often intentional teachers become champions for continuous improvement and advocates for educational equity. As teachers grow more intentional, they shift from asking "Why?" to asking "Why not?" They have the capacity to wrestle questions and debates with a mix of what they've learned from their own experience and from books, journals, and other publications. Intentional teachers may benefit from guidance and supervision, but they require less monitoring, because they monitor themselves.

> When teachers teach with a full awareness of what they are doing, better learning is the result.

Our focus on intentionality emerged as we reviewed the abundance of curricula, classes, books, and environmental props flooding the educational marketplace. It seemed to us sometimes that the ever-increasing number of educational materials aims to take the wisdom of teachers out of the teaching process. One teacher commented that some materials limit the teacher's role to delivering a "boxed" lesson. Another teacher referred to this trend as making teaching "idiot-proof."

We believe that teaching is so much more than that. It is an art and a science. We believe that a great teacher can compensate for limited materials and curriculum and imperfect environments. Conversely, even the best curriculum, materials, or environment may have only limited success if the teacher's skills and abilities are limited.

This book is informed by the sense that many of the resources aimed at teachers cater to materials and the environment—the tip of the teaching iceberg. The saying *the tip of the iceberg* refers to the obvious aspects of an object or situation, the part we can easily see. The saying implies that there is much more to an iceberg than its tip. What lies beneath the surface is wide, deep, and often undetected.

This book demystifies how to support the full development of teachers. It will help

A Teacher's Iceberg

Materials
(curriculum, assessment tools)

Environment
(room arrangement, placement of materials)

A teacher's behavior

A teacher's capability

A teacher's beliefs and values

A teacher's identity
(as a person and as a teacher)

A teacher's sense
of purpose

Adapted from Sylvia Guinan, "Why Do Teachers Teach?" August 15, 2013, www.wiziq.com/teachblog/why-do-teachers-teach.

you see and address the whole teaching iceberg. If you are a teacher, the chapters can guide your journey of self-discovery and self-determination. If you are supporting the development of teachers, this book can help you guide teachers toward creating and maintaining time for reflection, coaching, mentoring, and leveraging appropriate resources for the greatest good.

The Importance of Intentional Teaching in Early Childhood

Intentional teaching as a framework for teacher-directed professional development is fairly new to the early childhood field. We acknowledge that professional development can be challenging for early childhood educators. The field of early childhood education is broad and sometimes undefined, which makes development and implementation of effective professional development seem like an overwhelming task.

> In early childhood, educating and caregiving are intertwined. When you toilet train children, you are educating them. When you count up to ten with children, you are caring for them.

Early childhood teachers may enter the field through education or through caring for children in their homes. They work in a wide array of settings: child care centers, family child care homes, workplaces, churches, and schools. In each of these settings, teachers have varying time schedules, work patterns, resources, and leadership structures. Each setting has its own set of requirements, from Head Start performance standards to state licensing standards to teacher certifications and licenses. A teacher in early childhood may work with infants, toddlers, preschoolers, early elementary students, or all of these. Each age group requires specialized understanding of child development and age-specific instructional strategies.

In the past, early childhood education as a field has often seemed to have an artificial division between care and education. You can hear this in job titles of employees in the field. An early childhood educator could be called a child care worker, a teacher, a caregiver, or a provider. Meanwhile, all early childhood educators in all settings are involved in caring for and educating children. With young children, it is essential that teachers provide a nurturing relationship *and* an intellectually stimulating environment.

Some may believe a teacher's purposeful planning is more associated with children's intellectual development. With this view, some may feel that a discussion of purposeful instruction doesn't belong in early childhood professional development. However, teachers working with the whole child must use intentionality in all the areas of child development in order to be effective teachers. In addition, they do well to remember that in early childhood, educating and caregiving are intertwined. When you toilet train children, you are educating them. When you count up to ten with children, you are caring for them.

Given the diversity of settings, the broad array of job definitions, and the complexity of the job itself, it is imperative to address how early childhood teachers grow and develop in their profession. How do they learn to be more effective in their work with young children? Many current efforts in the field promote new content knowledge and teaching strategies. However, such efforts do not often address the development of each person's professional identity as a teacher. We see this as a missing element in the ongoing professional development experience for early childhood educators.

With evidence supporting the importance of the early years mounting, and with funding and attention increasing, discussion about early childhood professional development can't wait until the field is more standardized, more defined, or less conflicted. Young children need thoughtful, reflective, and purposeful teachers in all settings *now*, not at some indefinite point in the future. We hope this book serves you as an ally in your effort to become more thoughtful in your teaching—whatever your setting and job title may be.

Scope and Organization of This Book

This book is organized as a journey, starting with your first steps as a teacher.

Part 1: Starting the Journey

In Chapter 1 we explore the stages of teacher development, core beliefs on teaching, and how teachers change over time. Chapter 2 discusses intentionality and how it can help you navigate mandates, changes in expectations, and increased accountability.

Part 2: Change Brings Intentionality

Chapter 3 introduces the concept of a growth cycle that includes the following phases: Teachers Learn, Teachers Practice, and Teachers Share and Model. It lays the groundwork for Chapter 4, where we explore the first phase of the growth cycle, Teachers Learn. Chapter 4 also introduces the dimensions of teacher learning. Chapters 5 and 6 outline the next two phases of growth, Teachers Practice and Teachers Share and Model. How you balance observation and feedback with the realm of research, data, and standards—and the conflicting feelings that arise in the process— is at the heart of Chapters 4, 5, and 6. Purposeful and mindful instruction builds your teaching skills, confidence, and competence. It helps you achieve a balance in your practice. Chapter 6 outlines how you, armed with increased confidence, can create bridges to peers and families through modeling, presenting, and coaching.

Part 3: Getting What You Need

To continue your journey as an instructional leader, you must be equipped with the necessary tools. These tools include knowing yourself as a learner. In Chapter 7 you'll explore your learning styles and preferences so you can meet both your needs and those of the children in your care. Chapter 7 also explores the value of having support from a learning community or community of practice, mentors, and resources.

Chapter 8 addresses the questions, challenges, and problems you may face as you travel on your journey to intentionality. It begins with an approach to problem solving and follows up with an exploration of common problems. Chapter 9 discusses the importance of reflection and continuous improvement, and it features one teacher's journey to intentionality. It closes with a few words of encouragement from us to you.

Each chapter also includes:

▸ **Teacher stories.** These stories relate the experiences of teachers as they have gone through the changes we describe in the book. Some are direct quotes; others are composite stories. We appreciate the willingness of teachers to share their voices with us and illustrate our observations.

▸ **Reproducible forms.** We include forms at the end of chapters to help you explore your own personal reaction to the material. You can use these forms for reflection, to document and see progress and change during your journey, and as planning tools for the future. You can use the forms on your own, or you can use them with a peer teacher or mentor teacher, to discuss what you are learning. You can use and reuse the forms to notice where you are and how you are changing and growing or to set some direction for yourself when you are feeling confused or unsure. Please feel free to use these forms as you see fit.

You can access them from the book or download them as printables (see page 200 for details).

A note on language: When we use the term *teacher* in this book, we are referring to every adult in all early childhood settings—not only those with the "teacher" job title, but also family child care providers, assistant teachers, educational aides, paraprofessionals, and anyone else who comes into contact with the children in early childhood programs. Children benefit when all the adults who care for them become more intentional in their interactions and teaching activities.

Throughout this book, from example to example, we alternate between male and female pronouns to denote teachers and students. We recognize and value that both men and women are early childhood educators. And, of course, we acknowledge the gender diversity of children.

> Let this book be an ally in your effort to become more thoughtful in your teaching, whatever your setting and job title may be.

Finally, you will note that many of the examples we share from our own experiences relate to math learning. We use these examples to illuminate the concepts of intentionality. But of course, fostering language development, social-emotional learning, and other areas of learning also readily apply.

How to Use This Book

This book is a guide to help you recall how you came to the journey of teaching and to help you identify where you are in that journey. You'll find chapters dedicated to the twists and turns in the journey that may challenge you to rethink your choice of profession or your place in it.

This book is also a resource meant to encourage you to use a developmental framework when examining your professional growth. As a teacher, you are an adult learner, and your teaching knowledge and skills develop over time. *How* you learn affects what you are able to learn, revise, retain, and master. When you understand yourself as an adult learner, you can name what you need to learn. This leads to being able to ask for what you need and to being clear about what you don't find useful. It helps you be focused.

In this book we do not define or outline what you should do. The book is meant to be used for your own self-development as an educator. You need not read straight through it in order to benefit from it. You can sample it as you like, using the table of contents to guide your reading. You might skip around to chapters that help you at any given time or simply read the chapters in the order that interests you. Or you may want to explore the reproducible forms before reading the book. We encourage you to use this as a resource in a way most helpful to you. Whether you are a seasoned professional, a newly certified teacher embarking on your first tour of duty, or an educator somewhere in between, you'll find a wealth of reference materials, self-assessments, and conversation guides to appeal to a range of learning styles and levels of experience.

You may also use this book in your partnerships with other early childhood practitioners. If you participate in a learning community or community of practice with other early childhood educators, you may use the reproducible forms as individual reflection tools that can lead to group dialogue on approaches to teaching and learning. If you work with a coach or mentor, you may use tools from this book with your coach or mentor to deepen your understanding of each other's stories as you focus together on your teaching practice. If you are a program coordinator, you may wish to use some of the forms to stimulate conversations about the relationship between program philosophy and individual beliefs and practices.

However you use our book, we would love to hear your stories, thoughts, and comments. Tell us about your experiences and how you have developed as a teacher. Please contact us at help4kids@freespirit.com.

Welcome to the journey.

Sandra Heidemann
Beth Menninga
Claire Chang

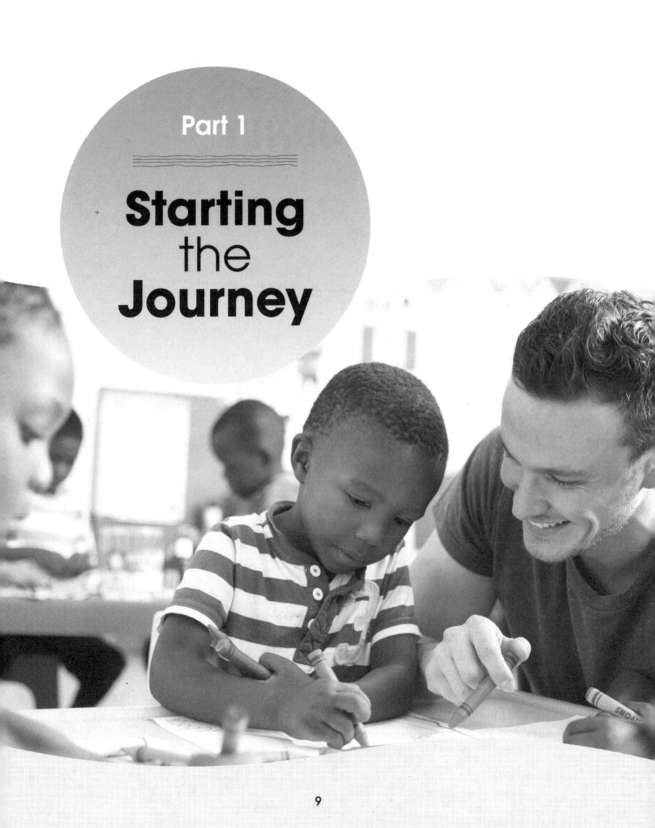

Part 1

Starting the Journey

1 TEACHING IS A JOURNEY

Here are several ways in which your development as a teacher is like a journey:

- It requires planning.
- It may be rocky at times.
- It may require adjustments to new environments.
- It may require learning a new language.
- It may involve detours or take unexpected twists and turns.
- It requires maps and assistance from others.
- It involves taking risks.

However, there is one big difference between your professional journey as a teacher and any physical journey you might take. A physical journey has a destination. But as a teacher, you are not really looking ahead to a specific destination. Instead, you are a lifelong traveler. You are constantly learning and improving as a teacher.

Teachers begin their journeys in a variety of ways, and their subsequent paths follow different routes. But all teachers develop skills, gain experience and knowledge, and form a philosophy of teaching as they travel along. The journey of teaching can bring you great rewards. You form deep relationships with children. You see how your daily efforts contribute to children's future success. You form partnerships with families to meet the needs of their children.

Teaching young children is a multifaceted task. You have to understand child development and curriculum content, pay attention to how children learn best, and evaluate the results of your work.[1] In one study of an early childhood professional development initiative, researchers found two striking phenomena. First, they found that effective early childhood instruction is more complex than most people think. Second, the researchers found that despite this complexity, many teachers are capable of learning it.[2] Your path as a teacher is more difficult than you may have thought, but it is also more accessible and more gratifying.

> As a teacher, you are a lifelong traveler. You are constantly learning and improving.

This chapter explores several factors that influence your teaching journey. First you'll think about how you began it. You'll look at the stages of teacher development to understand how your teaching experiences influence your professional development. You'll think about your core beliefs about teaching and learning. Once you have articulated your core beliefs, you'll explore the numerous changes you are asked to make in your work. What happens to your journey when, for example, you encounter a new curriculum, increasing standards, or an early literacy initiative?

The Journey Begins

Dionne had just received her child development associate (CDA) certificate and was proudly showing it to her family. She thought about her start in teaching. Her daughter had been in Head Start as a four-year-old, and Maria, the director, suggested she apply to be an aide in the classroom. Dionne didn't know if she could work with young children all day, but decided to apply. She found she was really good with young children and just kept working her way to assistant teacher. Now she wants to get her associate's degree at the community college.

Lauren had gone to college and majored in sociology. She wasn't sure what she would do with her degree and floundered when she got out of college. Finally, she found a job in a child care center as an aide. She found the work challenging and decided to take courses toward a degree in early childhood education. She loved the enthusiasm of the children and appreciated how hard the other teachers worked at the center.

Pedro entered college knowing he wanted to work with young children. Despite several people telling him he wouldn't earn enough in that profession, he chose a major in early childhood education. He graduated and found work in a kindergarten readiness program through a public school. He was excited to start his job, meet his new students, and plan instruction for the new school year.

These stories illustrate how teachers begin their careers in unique ways. While some of us realized at a young age that we wanted to teach, others were "accidental tourists" who meandered into the classroom and decided to stay. However you began your teaching career, reflecting on your beginnings gives you perspective on how important this work is to you, how invested you are, and where you are on your journey. Here are a few questions to ponder while reflecting on how you began:

▶ When did you first know you wanted to become a teacher?

▶ How did you feel at first, when you started teaching?

▶ What stands out about that first year (or month)?

▶ What did you learn about teaching young children that first year (or month)?

▶ What did you learn about yourself as a teacher that first year (or month)?

▶ What made you stay in early childhood education?

Fill out the reproducible form "Reflections on Beginning My Teaching Journey" at the end of this chapter (pages 22–23). Think about who you were when you began teaching and what you wanted to accomplish. When you think back, you may appreciate how many changes you have undergone since then. Even if your first experience was only six months ago, you will benefit from revisiting your early days.

Stages of Teacher Development

As you think back to your earliest days as a teacher, what pictures come to mind? You may remember a special child or a mentor who supported you. You may remember some lessons that did not work or times when children got excited about a book or science experiment. These memories are just the beginning of your story. Each year you teach, you have a distinctive experience with the children, your setting, your colleagues, and your own changing practice—all of which influence how you develop as a teacher.

To help us understand how teachers develop their skills and professional identity, let's examine two models. In the 1980s, Stuart and Hubert Dreyfus developed a five-level model of how professionals acquire skills.[3] In this model, the Dreyfus brothers break down the activities involved in acquiring skills and how these activities help professionals advance their technical and professional capabilities. In the second model, Lilian Katz examines how preschool teachers develop as they move through their careers.[4] Teachers go through stages in their careers that help determine what kinds of supervision, training, and support they need in each stage.

Dreyfus Five-Level Model

Think of all the skills you need in order to teach young children. You need to know how to set up an environment, choose materials, lead a group, manage transitions, write effective lesson plans, and do ongoing assessment. No one walks into an early childhood setting knowing how to do it all. If you envision teaching as a set of skills teachers learn in order to teach effectively, the Dreyfus model helps you break down the steps of that learning process. Breaking down the steps is helpful for teachers because it gives a clearer view of how teachers will reach their goals. It's helpful for supervisors, trainers, and instructors because it offers a way to match a teacher's training to what the teacher needs at each stage. The Dreyfus model outlines five levels through which a learner moves from novice to expert.*

- ▶ **Novice level:** The learner needs explicit rules and directed guidance.

- ▶ **Advanced beginner level:** The learner still needs rules to follow but now understands the context from considerable experience.

- ▶ **Competent level:** The learner knows the skills well enough to design goals, a plan, and strategies for when and how to apply rules and procedures.

*Gloria Dall'Alba and Jörgen Sandberg, "Unveiling Professional Development: A Critical Review of Stage Models," *Review of Educational Research* 76, no. 3 (2006), 383–412. Reprinted with permission of *Review of Educational Research*. All rights reserved.

▶ **Proficient level:** The learner is able to assess each new situation against a backdrop of previous experience.

▶ **Expert level:** The learner can identify problems, goals, plans, and actions; does not rely on explicit rules; and can help others learn the material.

These five levels track how a learner gains both skills and confidence. Think about your first day as a student teacher or an aide in a classroom. You may have felt like a novice. You probably remember wanting someone to just tell you what to do. Maybe the lead teacher asked you to work with an individual student or gave you a book to read with a small group. Eventually, with more training and experience, you become more able to address a wide variety of students and content areas. You can predict student reactions and responses based on what you have observed in the past. Your planning incorporates these observations and experiences and, more than likely, you successfully engage children in the activities you plan. As you reach the expert level, you can become a mentor to younger or less experienced teachers.

Let's examine one essential skill for early childhood teachers, *group instruction*, and see how it develops according to this model. Early childhood teachers need to be able to lead large groups of fifteen to twenty children in singing, learning concepts, or discussing various classroom issues. Group times cannot be too long or the children lose interest. But group instruction needs to be long enough to cover the material adequately. The chart on page 15 illustrates how the Dreyfus model breaks down the process of a teacher who's growing increasingly skilled at leading groups.

Katz Model of Teacher Development

Lilian Katz looked closely at how early childhood teachers develop over the course of their careers. She identified four stages through which teachers progress. She described each of the four stages and outlined the kinds of training and professional development most helpful for each stage.[5] Her descriptions fit closely with many teachers' experiences. Following are Katz's four stages.

▶ **Stage I—Survival:** Teachers in this stage may wonder, "Can I get through the day? Can I get through the year?" They feel anxiety and confusion and they doubt their abilities. They may wonder about their

Group Instruction Skill Development: Dreyfus Model

Level	Teacher's Behavior	How Teacher Learns Skill	Support Needed
Novice	Doesn't lead large group	Assists during group time Works with individual children	Directions on how to help children during group Activities to do with individual children
Advanced beginner	Doesn't lead large group	Assists during group time May help individual children listen during group, using a variety of techniques, such as sitting close to child, holding child on lap, and bringing attention to an activity	Nonverbal cues from teacher to know when to help a child Discussion with teacher about children's behavior and what helps them
Competent	Leads a section of a large group	Leads a segment of a group activity that is planned and time-limited, such as reading a book or leading a song Finds it hard to adapt to change in plan	Discussion with teacher about what book to read or song to sing, ensuring the book or song is enhancing the curriculum
Proficient	Leads whole group	Will plan and lead large group Can adapt plan if children lose interest or want to go deeper into material	Collaboration with fellow teachers to discuss goals and activities
Expert	Leads large groups Trains and supports others as they learn to lead large groups	Plans and leads large groups, easily adapting to changes Leads group instruction with consistently high quality Constantly finds ways to improve children's learning through this learning format	Encouragement to train others Collaboration with others to discuss goals and plans

competence. At this stage, teachers need support and encouragement. They should receive on-site instruction in specific skills.

▶ **Stage II—Consolidation:** Teachers use the knowledge they gained the first year to form a foundation. They are more able to see beyond the immediate daily demands to future needs. They often seek out information and support to help them serve individual children who are having difficulty. On-site training with a wider array of information and resources continues to be valuable. For example, teachers may find a meeting with a speech therapist to discuss the needs of an individual child very helpful.

▶ **Stage III—Renewal:** After a few years of teaching, teachers begin to tire of doing the same things over and over. They begin to ask questions about current trends and ideas. They seek out new resources for instruction by attending conferences, meeting with colleagues, and sharing ideas.

▶ **Stage IV—Maturity:** After three to six years of teaching, teachers reach the stage of professional maturity. At this stage, they feel confident in their abilities and are asking deeper questions, such as "What is my philosophy of teaching?" and "How can I teach more effectively?" Teachers at this stage do well if they can attend professional conferences, participate in a professional learning community or community of practice, or form a close relationship with a mentor, a supervisor, or a small group of fellow teachers with whom they can discuss these deeper questions.

After reading the description of Katz's model, which stage do you think you are in right now? Teachers can move forward and backward between stages when circumstances change. Sometimes even teachers with many years of experience can get thrown into the survival stage again. For example, in past workshops we, the authors, have presented Katz's framework to teachers and asked them what stage they thought they were in. One teacher shook her head and said, "I've been teaching a long time, but I just started in Head Start and I feel like I am back in the survival stage." Another teacher said she felt she was back in the survival stage because she had a group of children who were very active and challenging her authority.

Reflection and Transformation

Although the Dreyfus and Katz models do not align with each other exactly, if you place them side by side, you get a fuller picture of how you develop as a teacher. The chart below merges the two models.

Teacher Development Models: A Comparison		
Katz Model	Dreyfus Model	Differences and Similarities
Survival stage	Novice and advanced beginner levels	Katz's stages begin with first-year teachers; the Dreyfus model begins with staff at entry level in the field, such as aides and assistants.
Consolidation stage	Competent level	Both models describe teachers comfortable with teaching but needing support to keep developing skills.
Renewal stage	Proficient level	Katz describes teachers needing more professional development or a challenge to renew their interest in teaching; Dreyfus describes teachers who are more proficient because they have gained more skills.
Maturity stage	Expert level	Both models describe teachers as mature professionals willing and able to share their expertise with others.

Considering both of these models can help you identify your own stage of development. Reflecting on what stage you are in right now can help you make sense of your feelings and identify your needs. For instance, you might realize that a new set of expectations is making you feel like a beginner who needs everything spelled out. These models also show you that such a reaction to learning a new skill set is natural. You may feel like an expert or a mature teacher in one area of your practice, and that you are still becoming competent, or consolidating your practice, in another area.

Moving through the five levels or four stages of teacher development requires more than just gaining additional information and experience. It is a process of reflection and transformation. This transformation is not a simple linear line from one step to the next. It requires reflecting on how you think and feel about a content area, about children's learning, and about how best to engage children. Researchers and teacher educators Jörgen Sandberg and Gloria Dall'Alba describe how teachers develop within the context of changing expectations:

▶ You change how you see your role as teacher and how you teach.

▶ You change your beliefs about how children learn.

▶ You change how you interact with your environment and tools, such as your classroom setup and materials.

▶ You change your relationships with your coworkers, families, and supervisors.[6]

Moving through these stages can be stressful at times. However, reflection on your growth and the changes you have experienced also makes teaching a fascinating profession. Use the reproducible form "The Stage I'm In" on page 24 to reflect on the stages of teacher development you're in and how they affect your teaching practice.

Core Beliefs About Teaching .

As an adult, you have many facets to your identity. You may be a mother, a father, a daughter, a son, an uncle, or an aunt. When someone asks you, "What do you do for a living?" you likely answer, "I teach" or "I am a teacher." Being a teacher is a major facet of your identity.

Identifying your core beliefs about teaching is key to understanding who you are as a teacher. Your core beliefs are the inner values that help you make ethical decisions, plan lessons that engage children, and decide what will be in your learning areas. You form your core beliefs through your education, your training, your mentors, and most importantly, from your observations and experiences with children. Sometimes your core beliefs come from your own education as a child or deeply held values from your family. Then you build on core values from your childhood through your ongoing educational experiences.

It's a sign of healthy identity development when children bring their full selves to school every day: their home language and culture, their whole family, their community, their joys, their worries, all of it. When you as a teacher bring your whole self, including your beliefs and values, to work every day, you model authenticity to your students and their families.

What are your core beliefs? How do you stay true to your beliefs while honoring the diverse values of the children in your care and the program you work in? The reproducible form "My Core Beliefs" (on pages 25–26) will help you define what your core beliefs are. Knowing what makes you tick as a teacher provides an inner compass to help you steer on the road ahead.

How Have You Changed?

It takes time, experience, and reflection to become a skilled teacher. And teachers continue to grow and develop, because they learn as they teach. If you have been teaching for more than a few years, your core beliefs may have changed over time. You may have changed the way you lead groups or organize your transitions. You may intervene more quickly if you see a child with special needs or intervene less quickly when children are having a conflict during play.

> When you as a teacher bring your whole self, including your beliefs and values, to work every day, you model authenticity to your students and their families.

Many factors shape your teaching practice, core beliefs, and working knowledge over time. Some influences are so gradual that you hardly notice them. Others are abrupt and often brought about through outside initiatives or a big change in how your workplace is run. Here is a list of factors that can trigger changes in your beliefs and practice:

- a change in your workplace
- new experiences or experiences that contradict your expectations
- responses from children
- watching or working with other adults
- observations or assessments
- partnerships with families
- standards for teaching and learning
- input from supervisors, mentors, or coaches

Core beliefs have a powerful hold on how you teach. You may not even realize how deeply you hold these beliefs until they are challenged.

Sometimes, you may react negatively to such a challenge without understanding why. For example, how teachers interact with children in the classroom is a much-discussed issue in early childhood education. Traditionally, educators have been taught that young children should guide their own learning in the classroom with only minimal involvement from teachers. However, research has shown the value of teaching early literacy and numeracy in a new and different way. At times this new knowledge has required more explicit instruction to support children's learning. This change challenges teachers to fit what they already believe with new information about teaching young children.[7]

Derrick went to a university to get his teacher's license in early childhood education. He learned about developmentally appropriate practice[8] and strongly supported it. He wanted to reflect developmentally appropriate practice everywhere in his classroom. He felt children learned best when they directed their own learning. So he set up a stimulating learning environment and helped facilitate his students' learning.

However, in the last few years he has started to question the practice of self-directed learning. After learning more about how children develop literacy and math skills, he has changed the way he teaches. He still reserves a significant amount of time for children to explore the environment, but he is more aware of the important role he plays in helping children build on what they discover. For example, he asks questions that challenge children to talk aloud about their planning in the block area. He has added several activities that are more teacher-directed. In his large-group instruction, he teaches letter names and sounds with music. He also has made math games to include in his free playtime. He sits with his students as they play the games and asks questions, such as "How many more to reach the end?" He makes sure he uses lots of math language as they learn to play the games.

Derrick has found himself energized by the students' responses and the classroom assessment results. Now he believes it is important to use a mix of learning formats and methods depending on the composition of his group and the time of the year.

If you have been teaching for more than a few years, you too have probably seen many changes. The changes are not just coming *at* you; they are happening *inside* you as well. Whether you adopt or resist these changes, in the process of reflecting on these new demands, you become a different teacher. Your beliefs may be reinforced, may evolve, or may be discarded. In reflecting on research or new instructional practices, you broaden your outlook, knowledge, and core beliefs.

The reproducible form "How Have You Changed?" on page 27 gives you an opportunity to reflect on recent changes in your instruction. Complete the form and think about how these changes have informed your teaching journey.

This chapter illustrates how much goes into your identity as a teacher, including how you began your career, your developmental stage as a teacher, your core beliefs, and how you have changed. Most days, you are probably too busy to do this kind of reflection. Teachers often don't have much time to spend thinking. They are preparing lessons, doing assessments, going to staff meetings, meeting with families, and, of course, teaching children. At the end of the day, you just want to get home to attend to responsibilities there. However, we encourage you to set aside time to remember what you know about yourself as a teacher and to ponder what you have learned. Even spending a short amount of time thinking about your teaching journey will give you new insights and help you become a more thoughtful and deliberate teacher.

References

1. Susan H. Landry, Jason L. Anthony, Paul R. Swank, and Pauline Monseque-Bailey, "Effectiveness of Comprehensive Professional Development for Teachers of At-Risk Preschoolers," *Journal of Educational Psychology* 101, no. 2 (2009): 448–465.

2. Herbert P. Ginsburg, Rochelle Goldberg Kaplan, Joanna Cannon, Maria I. Cordero, Janet G. Eisenband, Michelle Galanter, and Melissa Morgenlander, "Helping Early Childhood Educators Teach Mathematics," in *Critical Issues in Early Childhood Professional Development*, eds. Martha Zaslow and Ivelisse Martinez-Beck (Baltimore: Paul H. Brookes Publishing Company, 2006): 171–202.

3. Jörgen Sandberg and Gloria Dall'Alba, "Returning to Practice Anew: A Life-World Perspective," *Organization Studies* 30, no. 12 (2009): 1349–1368.

4. Lilian G. Katz, "Developmental Stages of Preschool Teachers," *Elementary School Journal* 73, no. 1 (1972): 50–54.

5. Ibid.

6. Sandberg and Dall'Alba, "Returning to Practice Anew."

7. Landry et al., "Effectiveness of Comprehensive Professional Development for Teachers of At-Risk Preschoolers."

8. "Developmentally Appropriate Practice," NAEYC, 2009, www.naeyc.org/DAP.

Reflections on Beginning
My Teaching Journey

If you are new to the classroom, use this form as a way to document your current experience. Fill in as much information as you can. Plan to revisit what you have written at the end of your first year to make additions and to reflect on your year. If you are an experienced teacher, think back upon your first year of teaching to complete this form.

I first knew I wanted to become a teacher when . . .

During my first year of teaching, I felt . . .

A memory that stands out from my first year of teaching is . . .

During my first year of teaching, I learned that young children . . .

Here's what I learned about myself as a teacher . . .

After my first year, I decided to stay in early childhood education because . . .

The Stage I'm In

You may feel that you are at different stages in different areas of your teaching practice. For example, using a new assessment system may make you feel a bit incompetent (novice level or survival stage), while you feel that you could teach others in planning daily transitions (expert level or maturity stage). Try to find an example from your own practice for each stage and think about what might be helpful for you in each area.

Stage	Needs	Stage	Needs
Survival stage (Katz) Novice or advanced beginner level (Dreyfus)	Clear rules Concrete information On-site mentoring	Consolidation stage (Katz) Competent level (Dreyfus)	Workshops On-site mentoring Practice (including planning and goals)
I feel that I'm in this stage when:	**Something that might help me at this stage:**	**I feel that I'm in this stage when:**	**Something that might help me at this stage:**
Stage	Needs	Stage	Needs
Renewal stage (Katz) Proficient level (Dreyfus)	Diverse practice experiences Conferences Current research	Maturity stage (Katz) Expert level (Dreyfus)	Mentoring others Providing instructional leadership In-depth seminars
I feel that I'm in this stage when:	**Something that might help me at this stage:**	**I feel like I'm in this stage when:**	**Something that might help me at this stage:**

My Core Beliefs

I believe young children learn by:

One of the teacher's most important jobs is:

Curriculum in early childhood education should be:

I do assessment because:

Planning helps me:

One key to partnering with families is:

To continue growing as a teacher, I need:

In my interactions with children, I aim to be:

How Have You Changed?

Describe a change in your teaching that you've made in the last five years.

Why did you make the change?

How was the change prompted by an external requirement, research, or a workshop you attended?

How has this affected your experience as a teacher?

2 MOVING TOWARD **INTENTIONALITY**

Mai cleaned up the classroom after the children had left for the day. She thought about how her large group had gone. The children were restless, so she had done several music-and-movement songs and didn't get to the lesson she had planned on how plants grow. This restlessness continued the whole day. The children wandered around the classroom, and they got into fights during free play—a time when they were usually very engaged. It wasn't an easy day, and Mai felt a little discouraged. That evening she went to a workshop, and the presenter used the word *intentionality* several times. Mai wanted to learn more about this idea. She wondered, "What does it really mean to be an intentional teacher? How do I become one?"

Like Mai, you may have heard the word *intentionality* before. But you may not always know what it means for you in the classroom. If you are an intentional teacher, what would you do or say with children? Would it be different from what you do now?

Are You an Intentional Teacher?

Ann S. Epstein, in her book *The Intentional Teacher*, defines intentional instruction as having a goal and a purposeful plan to achieve it.[1] You think about what you teach in your curriculum, how you teach it to best engage the children, and how to tell if you have reached your goals. For example, if you want to bring more early math into your setting, you think about important concepts you want to teach, such as sorting materials into categories. You also think about what math language you want to use while teaching these concepts, what skills you want children to achieve, and how you'll evaluate their progress. In Mai's story, she *was* intentional when she planned the plant lesson for her large group. She also was intentional when she changed the plan because the children were restless. Mai adapted to the needs of the children. This flexibility to move back and forth between goals and planning and to adapt to the needs of the children requires observation, reflection, practice, knowledge, and ongoing assessment. In other words, being an intentional teacher means that you are growing consistently as a teacher, learning from any setbacks and detours you encounter.

Identifying the elements of intentional teaching is a complicated task, though, and teachers are often unsure when they are being intentional and when they aren't. A well-organized, busy classroom is not necessarily an intentional one. Robert Pianta has done extensive research on how teachers interact with children. He found that even when classrooms were well-organized and busy, they could be low in intentionality. He observed teacher-child interactions and determined that in some cases, they were not challenging, scaffolding, and extending children's skills in a planned way.[2] Without deliberate and purposeful interactions, children miss opportunities to deepen their learning. Here are some characteristics of intentional teaching to help you identify it in your own work:

> Being an intentional teacher means that you are growing consistently as a teacher, learning from any setbacks and detours you encounter.

- **You are knowledgeable.** You understand child development, and you know the early learning standards, individual content areas, and proven methods of instruction.

- **You have a relationship with each student.** You put great value on forming relationships with all the students in your classroom.

- **You adapt to new challenges.** You adjust your instruction to the different learning needs of students (including special needs), to new standards, and to new colleagues.

- **You plan from your goals.** You write goals based on your knowledge and the students' needs, and you plan activities and lessons to accomplish those goals.

- **You assess students and incorporate the assessment results in your planning.** You form your goals through your ongoing assessment of the children.

▶ **You reflect on your teaching.** You spend time evaluating how your lessons went, how students reacted to them, and how you would improve them. You regularly reflect on your assessment to determine if you have met your goals.

▶ **You do not give up.** You use problem solving to address challenges. These may be challenges with children or new areas of learning for yourself.

▶ **You see yourself as a lifelong learner.** You know you are always learning, and you offer others opportunities to be learners.

Examples of Intentionality

Components of Intentionality	Types	Examples in the Classroom
Planning and preparation	Lessons Studies and projects Themes Activities Environment	You spend time planning your themes. You prepare materials beforehand. You integrate content such as math and literacy into your lessons. You plan ways for families to become involved in their children's learning. Your environment reinforces children's learning.
Observation	Observing children Observing families Observing colleagues	You set aside time to observe children for assessment. You reserve time in your day to communicate with families about their children. You understand your colleagues' reactions and involve them in planning and assessment.
Goals	Based on assessment Based on knowledge of children Based on child development	You plan goals for each child. You plan goals for your class. You plan goals for your own growth as a teacher. You involve families in planning goals and help them understand their children's development.

Components of Intentionality	Types	Examples in the Classroom
Assessment	Authentic Ongoing Comprehensive Age-appropriate	You document the growth of each student. You learn how to gather data. You learn how to interpret data. You use data to plan goals. You reflect on data. You share assessment results with families. Your use of assessment is appropriate to the ages of the children in your setting.
Instructional formats and methods	Large group Small group Choice time Outside time Individualized instruction Routines and transitions	You use a variety of formats to engage children in learning. You balance adult-guided and child-guided learning. You integrate content such as math and literacy into all formats. You gauge children's interest and engagement in each format and adapt as needed. You reflect on how children were engaged. You seek out training.
Knowledge	Child development Special needs Research Specific content areas Teaching methods Cultural competence Developmentally appropriate practice	You have broad knowledge of child development. You have knowledge of special needs and how to adapt your methods to children's needs. You know how to engage young children in learning early math and literacy. You see yourself as a lifelong learner and consistently learn from your experiences and training. You seek out current research about young children and how they learn. You understand children within the context of their family, culture, and community.

The chart on pages 30–31 offers specific examples of intentionality that you may demonstrate—or develop—in your teaching. After reading the characteristics and examples, you may decide you are intentional in some areas and not in others. That's normal. We teachers are all constantly growing, changing, and becoming more conscious of our instruction.

Fill out the reproducible form "Intentionality Scale" on pages 43–44 to explore how purposeful you are in your teaching. Your responses on this form can help you set goals to develop more intentionality.

Learning Processes

The following paragraphs describe six learning processes: relationship, engagement, direction, reflection, ownership, and evaluation. You are probably already familiar with these six learning processes; you likely use them every day. By incorporating them into your daily lessons with children, you help children remember what you teach. When you pay attention to these processes, you are being a mindful, intentional teacher.

These processes are echoed throughout this book. Whatever tasks you undertake when you are teaching, you will use one or more of these processes.

Relationship

At the center of every teaching activity lies the relationship between the students and the teacher. This relationship is especially important for early childhood educators. Young children care deeply about their teachers and figure out quickly who cares for them. They learn best within a trusting and secure bond. What we may think of as small gestures—learning names, giving hugs, sharing laughter, listening carefully to long, involved stories—form the bedrock of connection for children. This connection in turn forms the foundation for taking risks, asking questions, and learning.

School and family form the center of a young child's world. So your relationships with families also affect the teaching and learning link. Building connections with families through regular communication, · newsletters, conferences, take-home activities, and family nights can help families reinforce lessons at home. When family members become partners with you, their children feel supported and encouraged.

Finally, your relationships with other adults in your program affect the children and play a role in your own learning. Adult interactions set the tone for classroom climates.

> Young children care deeply about their teachers and figure out quickly who cares for them. They learn best within a trusting and secure bond.

Engagement

Being engaged is getting involved in learning. Both teachers and children need to be engaged. As a teacher, you have to care about the subject area and the children you teach. You need to be curious about both what to teach and how to teach it. You must commit to follow-up and improvement.

Children are engaged when they are excited, seek out the activity, ask questions, and have fun. Lessons that incorporate engaging strategies and meaningful interactions for children will hold their attention. As a teacher, you can make certain that learning opportunities are hands-on and fun. You reinforce children's engagement through your comments, suggestions, and guided learning.

Direction

As a teacher, you have to know where you are going. You use your knowledge of child development, specific content areas, early learning standards, and your observations of the children in your classroom to set goals. If you realize that you have set your goals too high or too low, you can adjust the goals. Remember that even younger children benefit when you help them understand the goals of your learning activities. The way you share your learning objectives may be different than the way teachers of older children would, but this sharing serves the same function: helping children understand where they are going and when they have reached the goal. Sharing focuses their attention and thinking. For example, you may do a "picture walk" through a book before you read it to help children anticipate the plot. Or you may brainstorm a list of what the class may see on a future field trip and revisit the list after the field trip. Some curricula ask children to plan their activities in class and then talk about how the activities went.

Reflection

Reflection is perhaps one of the most important processes of both teaching and learning. Reflection helps you evaluate your goals, your strategies, your students' growth, and your own growth. It can be difficult to find the time to reflect beyond the in-the-moment reflection you do during an activity. But setting aside dedicated time to think about what you have done, the children's responses to it, and your own concerns about how a strategy went will keep you moving forward and focused on your goals. An effective teacher is a reflective teacher.

Ownership

As a teacher you are told over and over again what you should be teaching through curriculum, training, and standards. Supervisors, coaches, and mentors observe you and give you feedback. But in the end, you need to have ownership of what you are learning and how you teach children.

This means you take responsibility for continuing to learn and grow, and you apply that learning in your daily work with children and families. For example, when you are learning a new curriculum, you may worry that you are not teaching it exactly right. You may check your lesson plans to make sure you are including all components of the curriculum. As you gain more experience with the curriculum, you may experiment more with the schedule, activities, and environment based on your own comfort level, the responses of the children, and your teaching philosophy. You are going beyond what you are told to do. You are making that curriculum your own. When you are learning, and when you own what you are learning, you are bound to be more excited about teaching.

Evaluation

Ongoing evaluation is the basis of continuous improvement. As a teacher, you evaluate children's progress, both short-term and long-term. You gauge your own effectiveness as a teacher and seek to improve as you are able. As you grow in your professional skills, you evaluate how you share with your colleagues, model classroom activities, and interact with your director or principal.

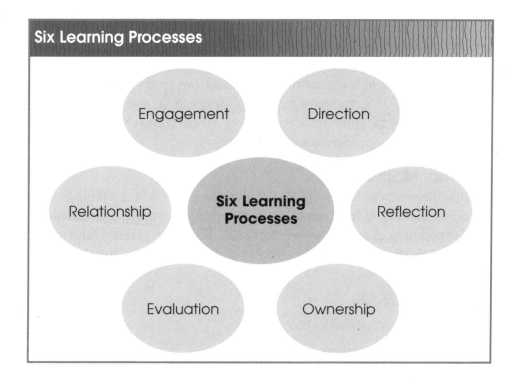

What Does Change Have to Do with Intentional Teaching?

Change can push you to become more purposeful. The impetus for change may be either internal or external.

Internal Motivators

Sometimes you become more purposeful after reflecting on your teaching or on your ideals and values. This kind of change begins within you; it happens because of internal motivators. For example, when you began teaching, you may have had an ideal teacher in your mind. This role model may have been someone you know, a teacher you once had, or perhaps an image based on a combination of teachers you have worked with who reflect your values. As you experienced the realities of teaching, you had to adjust your understanding of what makes a good teacher. But that ideal continued to motivate you. You grew in intentionality as you aimed for a clearer ideal.

Another internal motivator is your commitment to providing the best possible educational experience to the children in your classroom. As you learn more about how children learn, you change how you work. Because you want children to learn the most they can from your teaching, you take note of effective strategies supported by research, and you use them. These changes, too, come from within you—from your reflection on your experiences and your increasing knowledge.

External Motivators

Meanwhile, external forces are also challenging you. You can probably list the adjustments you have made in your teaching recently due to changing requirements from school boards, directors, licensors, trainers, and state standards. Here are just a few examples of the changes you may have had to implement:

- different curricula
- shifts in program leadership
- revised job descriptions
- different workplaces
- added responsibilities
- new or revised standards
- new instructional strategies for early literacy and math
- new assessment requirements
- revised accreditation standards or quality rating scales
- evolving research on child development

Often these changes do not happen one at a time. Typically you are coping with multiple changes simultaneously. One teacher told us that teachers are always waiting for the next tornado. In other words, new demands by directors or principals are thrust on teachers, resulting in more training and scrutiny. These tornados also bring stress and turmoil. The teacher commenting about the tornado of change was probably resentful of the required changes at first. However, if she was able to move beyond the initial resentment and dedicate herself to learning the new information or skill, she may have found a renewed interest in teaching. Despite the stress caused by external forces, they can be an impetus for growth.

> Carmen had just come back from a teachers' meeting, where her director had outlined a new project for this year. Her center was seeking accreditation for the first time. As part of that process, it was going to change to a new curriculum and assessment. Carmen had been teaching there for seven years, and she loved the activities she had developed with her team. She had so many questions. Would she have to give up all those beloved activities? How would she do all these new things when she would be starting a new class of children in just a week? She knew she would have more training, but even that seemed overwhelming. She didn't want to say this to anyone at her center, but secretly she hoped this change would just go away after a while, just as many others had.

Carmen's experience is not unusual. Early childhood education has been under increasing public examination over the past decade as public awareness of the importance of the early years has grown. As programs sign up for accreditation and quality rating scales, teachers are asked to increase their instructional skills, and expectations for assessment and accountability continue to rise. New projects and opportunities offer resources to teachers, families, and children that they didn't have before. But it isn't easy for teachers to integrate such changes into their practice. External motivators for change often require teachers to continue what they are doing while also doing something different. Let's examine two common challenges for teachers—early learning standards and assessment—and discover how addressing them can increase skills.

> Despite the stress caused by external forces, they can be an impetus for growth.

EARLY LEARNING STANDARDS

Standards are written descriptions of what children should know and do. Standards are a guide to a teacher's planning, instruction, and assessment. Most U.S. states have written standards for kindergarten through twelfth grade. Many states have adopted the Common Core State Standards in math and literacy. Many U.S. states and Canadian provinces have also written and adopted early learning standards (or frameworks) as guides for early childhood educators.

Early childhood teachers often have several sets of standards to learn. When defined broadly, the term *standards* or *frameworks* means more than just the state and provincial early learning standards for children. If we understand standards as codified expectations for students, teachers, or programs, it becomes clear that early childhood teachers are actually juggling several sets of standards as they try to improve their practice. The following chart outlines some of the differences in the various standards.

Differences in Standards

Type of Standards	Description
Early learning standards	State and provincial early learning standards or frameworks
	Head Start Early Learning Outcomes Framework
	Common Core State Standards
	Content standards
Professional standards	State competencies for teachers
	Developmentally appropriate practice
	NAEYC Code of Ethical Conduct
Program standards	Quality rating scales
	Accreditation
	Head Start Program Performance Standards
	Licensing

The number and variety of standards you must meet may feel overwhelming. You might feel it is impossible to meet all of them. However, when you use standards as a guide to your work (and at the same time, try not to view them as an imposition), they can increase your competence as a teacher in the following ways:

Standards help ground your curriculum. If you are familiar with what we expect children to know and be able to do at given ages, you have a framework to respond to the interests and questions of the children with whom you work. You are able to bring your knowledge about potential next steps in development as you scaffold on what children explore through studies, play, conversation, or other learning experiences.

Standards help you structure your assessment. When you know the standards, you can design small, quick assessments to see the progress children are making. You can also observe for growth in the more sweeping categories, such as social-emotional development. When you are assessing in this way, the standards help you observe children in more authentic settings, instead of evaluating them only via testing.

Standards help you observe children and their responses. You can see how children meet the standards throughout the day—in routines, during free play, during large and small groups, and during mealtimes. While you may sometimes also do more formal observations, standards help you see children's progress in different ways.

Standards help you evaluate your effectiveness as a teacher. By using the standards as a measuring stick, you can see how your strategies are affecting the children in your setting and consider ways to further scaffold their learning or provide support to promote their learning.

> ## How Do You Use Standards?
> Consider the following questions about the standards in your program. Thinking through these questions will help you use the standards in a more purposeful way.
>
> - What standards are you using in your program?
> - Which of the standards are most important to you?
> - How do you prioritize the standards?
> - What do you find most difficult in meeting them?
> - How do you explain the standards to families in your program?

The number of standards can be daunting. You probably have learning objectives for children in all developmental areas, and you may think it is impossible to address them all in one year. Reflect on your day and consider how you meet standards throughout the time children are with you. You will likely realize you are addressing standards by how you interact with the children, how you plan activities, and how you structure your routines. Carrying out standards can increase your effectiveness in the classroom.

ASSESSMENT

Programs and funding sources are asking for more and more assessment of young children and their learning. Although you may groan at the amount of paperwork and observation required to complete the assessments, they can also work *for* you as a teacher.

Early childhood educators use a variety of assessments. They range from short developmental checklists to observations to collecting samples of children's work. Using a variety of methods to capture the many ways young children are learning is key to assessment. Aim for authentic assessment, a method of assessing children in a natural setting, rather than setting up a more artificial situation, such as a test. Authentic assessment means you observe children as they play or during large and small groups. Young children can be difficult to assess because they are often distracted or uncooperative. So doing assessment over time captures a more accurate picture of a child's skills. Assessment over time means you document what children are learning more than once.

> Assessment can be a valuable tool for you as a teacher. You can plan from the results, see individual children's progress, and gauge your own instructional effectiveness.

When you were growing up, you probably took tests at the end of units, quarters, and semesters. You may remember feeling anxious as the test dates approached. These tests often counted toward your grade in the class. Because of experiences like this, you may shy away from doing assessments, only reluctantly completing them when you are asked to do so by your program. However, assessment can be a valuable tool for you as a teacher. You can plan from the results, see individual children's progress, and gauge your own instructional effectiveness. According to *Principles and Recommendations for Early Childhood Assessments,* assessments have four main purposes:[3]

- to support learning
- for identification of special needs
- for program evaluation and monitoring trends
- for high-stakes accountability

Of those four purposes, early childhood teachers mainly use assessment as a way to support children's learning. (In addition, programs often ask teachers to complete assessments for program evaluation and reports to funders.) Objective, reliable observation and assessments help teachers decide goals for individual and group curriculum content and determine how they want to approach the subject area and each individual child.[4]

Teachers learn about assessments by administering, analyzing, and planning from them. However, teachers face challenges as they are learning. As teachers learn more about conducting and planning from assessments, they often have questions. Here are some concerns teachers share:

- Sometimes teachers don't receive assessment results until the beginning of the next year. Classroom teachers lose valuable opportunities to respond to results when they cannot see how their students did on assessments in a more timely manner.

- Teachers may not have adequate computer skills (or sufficient technology) to complete the online assessments now being used in many schools and early childhood programs. When assessments are too frustrating to complete, teachers may not be as attentive to details or documentation.

- Teachers may not understand the process of planning from assessment results. Writing goals and planning strategies based on children's performance can be complicated, and teachers may not receive training or assistance to accomplish it.

- Assessments may not give teachers enough specific information about children's performance to help them set achievable goals. Broad, vague assessments may be simpler to complete yet harder to plan from.

Despite these challenges, good assessment is a critical tool. You can use assessments to help you improve your instruction so all children achieve their goals. If you recognize these challenges as part of your experience, seek out support. Other teachers may have faced similar situations and found ways to address them. Supervisors may schedule additional trainings or spend a staff meeting on assessment issues. If you feel you don't have the computer skills (or sufficient technology) to complete assessments, ask your director or supervisor for more help.

To explore how your understanding of assessment has changed during your teaching career, and how you might use assessment to better support your teaching in the future, fill out the worksheet "Changing Assessments" on page 45.

Moving toward intentionality, or learning to teach with a purpose in mind, brings benefits to everyone in your program. Increasing your intentional instruction not only helps children learn more, it also brings you more fulfillment as a teacher. The constant changes in the field of early childhood education can be frustrating, but they also offer you opportunities to grow in your abilities and your professional identity.

References

1. Ann S. Epstein, *The Intentional Teacher: Choosing the Best Strategies for the Young Children's Learning* (Washington, DC: NAEYC, 2014): 5.

2. Robert C. Pianta, "Standardized Observation and Professional Development: A Focus on Individualized Implementation and Practice," in *Critical Issues in Early Childhood Professional Development*, eds. Martha Zaslow and Ivelisse Martinez-Beck (Baltimore: Paul H. Brookes Publishing Company, 2006): 231–254.

3. National Education Goals Panel, *Principles and Recommendations for Early Childhood Assessments* (Washington, DC: U.S. Government Printing Office, 1998).

4. "Screening and Assessment of Young English-Language Learners," NAEYC, 2005, www.naeyc.org/files/naeyc /file/positions/ELL_SupplementLong.pdf.

Intentionality Scale

For each question, check the answer that best reflects how you function as a teacher.

Planning and Preparation	Always	Usually	Sometimes	Never
1. I plan and prepare my lessons ahead of time.				
2. I plan projects related to the children's interests and community opportunities.				
3. I coordinate the activities in the classroom with activities for families to do at home.				
Observation	Always	Usually	Sometimes	Never
4. I observe individual children and children as a group to gain information about the effectiveness of my teaching strategies.				
5. I observe children to discover their interests and strengths.				
6. I observe children as part of my assessment.				
Goals	Always	Usually	Sometimes	Never
7. I set goals and plan teaching strategies based on the data.				
8. I set goals to improve my own teaching skills.				
Assessment	Always	Usually	Sometimes	Never
9. I document each child's growth as part of an assessment.				
10. I interpret data on each child and for the group as a whole.				
11. I share my assessment data with families.				

Instructional Formats and Knowledge	Always	Usually	Sometimes	Never
12. I use large group, small group, choice time, and outside time to help children grow in each of the five domains: approaches to learning, social-emotional, physical, language, and cognitive development.				
13. I have knowledge of special content areas such as literacy, math, and science.				
14. I integrate these content areas into my daily schedule.				
15. I have studied child development and continue to learn from individual children.				
16. I seek out research to help me use the most effective ways to teach children.				
17. I seek out information about special needs and how a special need may affect a child.				

Look at your answers. To which questions did you answer "Always" or "Usually"? These are probably areas in which you feel very comfortable. To which questions did you answer "Sometimes" or "Never"? These are probably areas you want to address.

Set two goals based on your answers to help you develop more intentionality:

Changing Assessments

Think back on how you conducted assessments when you first started teaching.
How has your practice changed?

How I assessed then:

How I assess now:

Reflections on what changed, what I learned, and what's next:

Part 2

Change
Brings
Intentionality

3 CHANGE HAPPENS IN PHASES

Dominic laughs as he recalls the skepticism he felt when he first heard that his program was starting a new early math partnership. He says, "I thought I knew enough already about teaching math and didn't want to add more paperwork to my life. Everything in my classroom already looked really good, my group was engaged, and I *was* teaching some math, but I didn't always think about it from the kids' point of view. I think sometimes I overestimated what they were learning, and other times I underestimated what they could do. And at first I was worried we were going to expect the children to do things that weren't age appropriate.

"Still," Dominic continues, "I always like to learn new teaching ideas, so when we heard the math speakers share what they do with children, I was excited to try some of their strategies. I worked with my coach to try different math activities and saw how much my children loved them. The assessment showed me how much the kids grew in their counting skills.

"All of that has made a huge difference in how I think about math and how I teach. Last year we added a new routine using the estimation jar and number line, and my children just love it! I see them applying it to other things; like when they are playing, sometimes they'll use the number line to confirm a number or talk about who has more. This year I've been showing the estimation jar routine to other teachers at my site and they've been using it in their own ways in their classrooms."

The previous chapter discussed some changes that require you to stop and think about your teaching practice. Change can be a catalyst to help you become more purposeful in your teaching.

Change Spurs Growth

Although you might like your teaching journey to be straight and paved, all teachers face bumps, curves, and detours along the way. These bumps, curves, and detours challenge you to reexamine your practice and your beliefs about teaching. They provide new views and information, along with opportunities to try new tools or hone old ones. As a result, you may find yourself headed in a new or different direction. Changing direction can, in turn, kindle self-examination and new strategies and insights.

If you look back at your teaching career, you will see growth over the course of your career. But your growth as a teacher does not occur in a predictable, step-by-step fashion. Instead, you experience growth cycles spurred by change. These growth cycles give you repeated opportunities to explore and reflect on your teaching practice and increase your intentionality.

Chapter 1 discussed various experiences that may generate cycles of change. Taking on a new position or working in a new setting may prompt an intense period of growth. Facing new challenges with an individual child or group of children may stimulate a major rethinking of your approach to teaching or classroom management. New assessment information or changes in standards may prompt questions about how your teaching practice affects children's learning. All of these changes may spur growth in your teaching, but in this book we'll focus on how your experience with professional development leads you to instructional change.

> Bumps, curves, and detours challenge you to reexamine your practice and your beliefs about teaching.

Professional development initiatives often require you to learn new background knowledge and use new evidence-based teaching practices. This may mean integrating new information or strategies into existing strategies, or it may mean altering your teaching practice more extensively. Either way, you may find yourself approaching your work from a new perspective.

Professional development can inspire you to rethink your strategies and routines. You may ask yourself questions such as "Is this the right way to do this?" or "Do I need to adapt or change my approach?" or "What would happen if I . . . ?"

This is true for teacher trainers as well. Sometimes we have had to question our approaches to professional development when teachers questioned our suggestions based on their experiences.

Here is one example of rethinking practice from our work with teachers on early math. To introduce children to counting, we asked teachers to use homemade board games as a teaching tool to help children construct their own understanding of numbers. At first, we told the teachers not to set any game rules, so children could learn by developing their own rules. This was a new idea to teachers, who were used to teaching children the rules of games—but they were willing to try it.

The teachers soon reported that many children who had no exposure to board games didn't know how to begin. We had to rethink our approach. Instead of asking the children to make up the rules, we suggested that the teachers could model how to play with the game board. This spurred the teachers to make a change in their instruction. Through their modeling, they sent children the message, "Here is one way to play the game," without implying that the game had rigid rules. With this approach, game playing took off in many classrooms, and children had abundant opportunities to develop their own knowledge about numbers.

We and the teachers had come into this training thinking one way would work best, but through the obstacle we encountered, we found another way worked better—and still fit with our belief that children should construct their own understanding of numbers.

A Three-Phase Growth Cycle: Learning, Practicing, Sharing

When you are learning to integrate new information and practices into your teaching, you go through a three-phase growth cycle. Let's use an example from gardening to understand this common experience of teachers a little better. Experienced gardeners know that it takes patience to reap the rewards of perennial plants. They often encourage new gardeners to allow at least three years before expecting to see the true beauty of the plants. A common gardening proverb says, "The first year they sleep, the second year they creep, the third year they leap." A perennial plant in its first year appears to sleep as it gets rooted in the garden. Second-year perennials appear to creep as they begin to show growth in leaves and flowers. Third-year perennials seem to leap—sometimes becoming even bigger than expected—reseeding or spreading enough to create new plants for the garden.

We have observed a similar three-phase pattern among early childhood educators who are experiencing a change in their teaching practice. Over time, teachers move from learning new content to practicing the application in the classroom to sharing it with others. We've named these three phases as follows:

▶ Teachers Learn

▶ Teachers Practice

▶ Teachers Share and Model

Teachers Learn

In the following story, you will see how Marian learns new knowledge about the way children develop mathematical understanding. You'll also see how she explores the implications of this knowledge in her classroom.

Marian is an experienced Head Start teacher who has just begun a new school year. Her program is participating in two new initiatives, one of which focuses on early math. At this point, Marian is in her first year of the initiative. She is always interested in learning new knowledge and strategies, and she looks forward to expanding her math teaching skills.

However, she feels a bit like she is starting over as she tries new teaching strategies, which don't always work the way she expects. For example, after attending a training on using board games to develop number sense, she introduces a new board game. The game board is a simple, short path of ten spaces labeled with the numerals one through ten. Marian puts the game out with a single die and sits by as several children play with it a little, then leave the game on the table.

After watching a couple of girls play the game side by side, Marian realizes that the die she has provided, which is a standard die with dots from one to six, is making the game end quickly. Children often start the game with enthusiasm, but just toss the die around and move the counter and then leave the game. At first Marian wonders if the children are bored with the game. But after talking with her coach, she decides that the children aren't ready to use the one-to-six die. She creates her own die with only one dot or two dots on each side. She plays the game alongside the children, naming each space with its numeral label as a model for them. She also creates a new longer-path game with twenty spaces for children who can easily count the one-to-six dots on a standard die.

During the first phase of a growth cycle, teachers spend time learning new ideas about how children develop and learn. When learning about early literacy education, teachers wrestle with concepts of phonological awareness, such as how young children begin to understand what a rhyme sounds like. While learning about early math education, teachers like Marian delve into young children's counting strategies. Like a perennial newly planted in a garden, teachers establish their roots in new knowledge and explore its implications in the classroom.

Teachers Practice

In the second phase of Marian's story, you will see how Marian puts her new knowledge into practice. You'll also see how she analyzes the children's responses to her methods to learn more about how children develop mathematical understanding. She then uses this new learning to refine her practice.

> During her second year of participation in the early math initiative, Marian begins to feel more grounded in her teaching again. She feels as if she has a better understanding of children's development of numeracy skills. She has begun to use her observations of children's board game play to document their understanding of number concepts, such as *cardinality*. (The last number counted in a set of items represents the amount of items in the set.)
>
> Marian remembers that workshop presenters encouraged her to ask questions about how children decide "how many," so she could gain insight into their counting strategies. Her coach, too, has encouraged her to ask children, "How do you know?" after telling her how many objects they have. At first Marian felt a little awkward when she asked children this question. Now it is second nature and comes out naturally when she is not sure what strategy a child is using to determine an amount.
>
> Her coach notes that Marian has greatly increased the amount of math language she uses throughout the day. Marian feels comfortable threading math exploration into classroom studies. She is especially proud of integrating math into creative experiences. For example, her class completes a study of plants, and her students create a lovely garden mural for their classroom using a variety of geometric shapes.

During the second phase of a growth cycle, teachers put their new knowledge to practice. For example, Marian consciously works at using more math language throughout the day.

Teachers Share and Model

In the third phase of Marian's story, you will see how Marian gains enough experience and confidence to share her experiences with other teachers. You'll also see how, by sharing and modeling, Marian deepens her own knowledge.

> Now Marian is in her third year of the math initiative. Later this morning, she will help lead a workshop for other teachers. Marian nervously reviews in her head what she wants to say, because she doesn't want to forget her presentation. She plans to describe each step she took to integrate math concepts into her classroom's study of plants. She smiles as she recalls the pride children took in measuring and documenting the growth of their plants.
>
> After her presentation, Marian is pleased and a little surprised at the warm response and deep interest expressed by the teachers in her session. She reflects on some of the things she has learned from other teachers over the past few years and recalls how valuable some of those lessons have been to her own growth and learning.

In the third phase of a growth cycle, teachers gain more experience and confidence in their new knowledge and skills. They are ready to share their experiences with others. By doing so, teachers explore their new practice on a deeper level.

Marian's story demonstrates that as teachers grow more comfortable with content and practice, they are able to generate and share their own new strategies. Here are other examples:

- One teacher shared examples of how he had integrated the books children dictated and illustrated into the classroom library.

- Another teacher explained that he had begun using child-made labels in his classroom instead of creating his own.

- A third teacher invited others into her classroom to see children write the words inviting family members to family events, creating beautiful and meaningful invitations.

When teachers share with their peers, they spread the seeds of new ideas while fostering their own continued growth. Teachers can also model and share strategies with families. For example, they can share specific strategies tied to student assessment at conferences and home visits, model play at family fun events, and identify concepts in children's books at family workshops.

The chart on page 55 outlines the three phases of teacher growth. The timelines are fluid. They vary depending on how experienced teachers are, what supports they receive, and what teachers already know about the subject area. One teacher may move to modeling and sharing by the second year, while another is still integrating new ideas into the classroom during the third year. While some teachers might be able to fully implement a change in a shorter time, the three phases typically take at least three years. Over and over again, throughout our fourteen years of working with teachers on changing their instruction, we have found that supervisors and teachers usually underestimate the time and effort it takes to integrate instructional changes.

> As teachers grow more comfortable with content and practice, they are able to generate and share their own new strategies with peers and with families.

Each phase includes learning, practice, and sharing and modeling to a greater or lesser degree. But each of the three phases focuses on a particular developmental task. In the first phase, the developmental task is learning. The second phase centers on practice. The third phase focuses on sharing and modeling.

Studying this framework can help you understand how you gain more expertise and become more purposeful in your work with young children. This framework shapes our next three chapters, where we explore more deeply the three phases: Teachers Learn, Teachers Practice, and Teachers Share and Model.

Three Phases of Teacher Learning

Teachers Learn	Teachers Practice	Teachers Share and Model
About themselves:	**About themselves:**	**About themselves:**
Identify and adjust beliefs about teaching and learning	Deal with disequilibrium	Expand professional identity
	Raise more questions	Develop leadership and communication skills
Identify strengths and areas for growth	Take ownership for own learning	
Gain knowledge about teaching and learning:	**Deepen content knowledge:**	**Further deepen content knowledge:**
Learn new research, theory, and application	Try techniques, observe children's responses, adapt	Hone knowledge by describing and demonstrating
Consider how this affects own practice (for example: assessment, parent engagement)	Link assessment data and observations to practice	Develop new strategies, specialize
	Integrate knowledge into curriculum	
With others:	**With others:**	**With others:**
Develop new roles and relationships	Attend to group and individual responses	Share informally and formally in many ways
Try new ways of interacting	Attend to context	Become a teacher leader
	Partner with other adults	Use mentoring and supports from and provide mentoring and supports to others
Use mentoring and supports from others	Use mentoring and supports from others	
Potential dilemmas:	**Potential dilemmas:**	**Potential dilemmas:**
Facing conflicts with core beliefs	Struggling with application at a deeper level	Finding confidence to share with others
Experiencing disruption	Struggling with integration	Determining how and what to share
	Feeling disequilibrium	
Focus:	**Focus:**	**Focus:**
Learning new material and strategies	Exploring what children know and can do, how they respond, and what it means for own teaching practice	Forming a learning community or community of practice to support continued learning and practice
Coping with how that feels		

4 TEACHERS LEARN

Renee's Head Start program is beginning to use the Classroom Assessment Scoring System (CLASS)[1] observation tool to rate teacher-student interactions. As Renee begins reading a book to the children during the morning large-group time, she anxiously watches the observer who's in her classroom to rate interactions. Renee knows she is supposed to be building higher level thinking skills through conversations, but she feels unsure about how to carry out those conversations.

Kue attentively watches the video of a teacher describing and demonstrating concrete graphing strategies. The teacher in the video is graphing shoes and boots on a large floor graph made of felt. Kue feels his five-year-olds are ready to move from graphing with concrete objects to graphing with more abstract representations, such as pictures or symbols. His mind races with many ways he could introduce this approach to the children at his center.

Isobel secretly rolls her eyes as she tries to listen to the trainer introducing another social-emotional curriculum to the teachers in her preschool program. Isobel feels proud of how well she manages behaviors in her classroom. She resents the implication that her hard work is somehow not good enough.

Chapter 3 described the three phases of growth teachers experience as they engage in instructional change. This chapter will explore the first phase, Teachers Learn, and what it means for you.

Renee, Kue, and Isobel are all facing change. Each example of change is both an opportunity and a challenge. All three teachers stand at the beginning of a new experience, a situation that can bring up feelings of uncertainty and risk. When a teacher begins a new experience, he naturally wonders how this new adventure will affect him, what he will be expected to know and do, and how the experience will impact his interactions with children, families, peers, and supervisors. When you enter into a new teaching experience, you may have similar questions, such as:

- What am I going to have to do differently?

- How disruptive will this be?

- How will this affect the children in my classroom?

- How will it affect my workload?

- Will I be able to make this change?

There is often much to learn in this first phase of growth, and you might not be able to imagine how you will absorb it all. Entering into the unknown may be a little scary. But the more you understand about the learning process, the better you can face the uncertainties. Let's begin by thinking about what kinds of learning happen in this phase.

Dimensions of Learning

If you look at the teacher stories at the beginning of this chapter, you can see that each learning opportunity has multiple layers. For example, Renee is learning about promoting children's thinking skills through adult-child interactions. As she tries different strategies to develop thinking skills through her interactions with children, she learns from the children's responses and from her own reflections. Renee is also learning about a particular tool, the CLASS, which defines and measures these types of adult-child interactions. In addition, she is learning how to use feedback from observers of her teaching to improve her practice.

To help us understand such layers of learning, let's look at learning as a process with three dimensions. Researchers Sarah Mackenzie and George Marnik identify three dimensions of learning at work when you develop new skills: *intrapersonal* learning, or learning about yourself; *cognitive* learning, or learning about content and strategy; and *interpersonal* learning, or learning through interacting with others.[2] Intrapersonal learning is internal. It focuses on awareness of your own teaching philosophy, your teaching strengths and gaps, your personal learning styles and preferences, and your hot spots (issues that touch a nerve) and biases. Cognitive learning centers on theory and research about what and how children learn and on teaching strategies and how to use them effectively. Interpersonal learning focuses on working with others, including children, colleagues, families, supervisors, and administrators. Here is a chart linking each of these dimensions with examples:

Dynamic Dimensions of Teacher Learning	
Dimension	**Examples Related to Instructional Change**
Intrapersonal learning (learning about yourself)	My feelings and how they affect my work
	My beliefs and values about teaching, learning, children, and families
	My sense of myself as a teacher: what I do well, what I need to strengthen, my teaching style and preferences, hot spots or biases
	My learning style and preferences
Cognitive learning (learning about content and strategies)	What I already know and do
	What new information I am learning: theory, research, standards, procedures, and processes
	How to apply the new information in my teaching practice: instructional and assessment strategies, accountability to standards
Interpersonal learning (learning through interacting with others)	How this will affect my relationships with children, coworkers, families, and others
	How I might change my interactions with children

These dimensions will frame our discussion not only of teachers learning, but also of teachers practicing and teachers sharing and modeling. We will use this framework to deepen our understanding of all three phases of growth as we explore them in this chapter and the next two chapters.

Learning About Yourself

Learning about yourself means reflecting on your philosophy of teaching and developing awareness of yourself as a teacher. At the beginning of a new learning experience, you may question if this new approach or process will align with your beliefs about teaching. You may wonder what you will learn about yourself as a teacher. On the other hand, you may look forward to the challenge. If we look back at the teacher stories that lead off this chapter, and discover more about each teacher's situation in the following paragraphs, we see each teacher has a unique personal reaction to the proposed change.

Renee is reading to a group of children in front of a CLASS observer. As she reads, she realizes she does not feel confident managing deep conversation with children in a large group. She feels torn between having an extended conversation while keeping the large-group time under fifteen minutes, which she believes is the maximum time to spend in a large group.

Kue is excited about learning new strategies for teaching children about graphing. He has established good routines in his second year of teaching at his school, but he wants to challenge himself and the children in his classroom. He wants to start with a concrete graphing experience using real shoes, then move to using pictures of shoes in the graphs. The training video Kue watches says that moving from concrete to pictorial representation in graphing with children helps children make connections between hands-on learning and more abstract representations of ideas. This aligns with what Kue believes about best teaching practices.

Isobel is going to start a new social-emotional curriculum. Her responses reflect her many years of experience in her early childhood center. Her eye roll reflects her cynicism about new initiatives, because her program tends to follow one trend after another. Isobel feels frustrated because it seems that her supervisor doesn't value her skills in engaging students and managing her classroom.

For these teachers, change leads to reflection on their beliefs, values, emotions, and professional identities. It means taking the time to learn something new, expending extra effort, feeling uncomfortable while experiencing the unfamiliar, and making mistakes or struggling to regain a sense of routine or competence. Some teachers welcome the challenge that change brings—and may actually be pushing for change. Other teachers initially respond with a mix of resignation, resentment, and fear. They may feel off-balance during the learning and practicing phases of growth. These are all natural emotional responses to change.

One teacher recalled her reaction to the news of a new math initiative: "Oh boy! What are we getting into? My anxiety about math is high. I am not good at math. What am I going to have to teach, and what am I going to have to learn?" This teacher was generally confident in the classroom and interested in new ideas, but math was an uncomfortable area for her because of her own childhood math experiences. Her experiences shaped her emotional response to this new learning opportunity. Teachers may respond differently to change depending not only on their personal experiences, but also on their stage of teacher development.[3] A new teacher who is in survival mode (see "Katz Model of Teacher Development," pages 14–15) may not feel ready to take on changes. A mature teacher who may feel he has done his time and paid his dues may be uninterested in learning new content or strategies.

During the learning phase of growth, you may change your professional identity or your view of yourself as a teacher. Your confidence may be shaken. Change may bring feelings of confusion, loss of control, and even incompetence as you try new strategies or alter familiar routines. Most people do not like feeling vulnerable. Teachers, in particular, want to both show and pass along a sense of confidence to their students and families. Many teachers have already invested a lot of time and effort in learning how to teach, so it is natural that many teachers feel reluctant to change. Change means a teacher may have to rewrite the story of her teaching, adding new paragraphs to a script that feels just right.

> Some teachers welcome the challenge that change brings. Other teachers initially respond with a mix of resignation, resentment, and fear. These are all natural emotional responses to change.

Change can also challenge a teacher's values and beliefs about teaching and learning. New information may reinforce and enhance some beliefs and values while conflicting with others.

The context of change can shape your responses, too. How your organization or school has introduced and rolled out teacher development initiatives in the past influences how teachers respond. If your program has had several changes in leadership over a short period of time, you may feel distrustful at first. The rapidly shifting leadership may make you feel it's prudent to wait before you commit to a change, since administrators may switch direction again. If your program starts several new initiatives at the same time, you may feel overwhelmed with the new strategies, information, and changes you are expected to adopt simultaneously. Even if you are excited about learning new strategies, you may not be able to do it all at once.

Guiding Questions: Learning About Yourself

Here are some guiding questions to help you learn about yourself as you embark on change in your teaching:

> How can this experience build on your teaching strengths? How confident or nervous are you about your knowledge or skills in this area? If you are feeling uncertain, what worries you about your knowledge or skills?

> How does this new experience align with your teaching philosophy (your beliefs and values about teaching and learning)? Where does it conflict with your philosophy?

> How might this new experience bring up some of your hot spots or biases? What can you do to address possible hot spots or biases?

> What is the likelihood of your organization or school supporting you as you learn this new material?

If these questions raise concerns for you, think about ways to address them:

> You may have to live with ambiguity for a while, knowing that your concern may be resolved as you learn more.

> ❯ You may need to bring your concern to someone else who's in a position to address it.
>
> ❯ You may need to find a trusted ally (a coach, another teacher, or your supervisor) who knows you and is willing to serve as a critical friend through this new experience. Someone who is committed to your growth can be an excellent sounding board and provide valuable feedback through the process.

Intrapersonal learning, or learning about yourself, is about who you are as a teacher. While it is important to understand your feelings, your beliefs, and your reaction to change, it is also important to process the new content and strategies brought to you by this change. Learning about content and strategies, or cognitive learning, is about what you teach and how you teach it.

Learning About Content and Strategies

In this first phase of growth, you are learning about specific content areas, such as literacy, math, or science, which may be new to you. You are also learning how to teach this content through your classroom strategies and routines. If you are adopting new content standards, you are learning what those standards are and how you must apply them in your daily work.

When asked about this dimension of her learning, Renee defines the content she is learning as using conversation to develop higher order thinking skills. She attended a presentation that described research showing the powerful impact of this teaching strategy. Renee feels she still needs to learn more about how this strategy plays out in different teaching situations.

When asked about this dimension of his learning, Kue says that he's learning how children understand graphing and how he can teach graphing effectively. He is working to understand the content in two areas: what children are learning and the teaching strategies to support that learning. Kue feels this content builds comfortably on his existing knowledge of child development.

When asked about this dimension of her learning, Isobel says she is comfortable with the content she's learning. She has completed a lot of training on social-emotional development and feels confident in this area. She feels competent at completing her program's assessment system and noting student growth in social-emotional development. She wonders if this new curriculum's focus on self-regulation is the same information she already knows—or something new to learn.

These stories illustrate that learning new content and strategy is accessible when new knowledge builds on what you already know and understand. When this happens, you feel less overwhelmed. For example, one teacher explained, "Once I sat back and reevaluated, I realized I was doing math with the kids but didn't realize it. The work is not way out there and big—it's small and reachable."

This dimension of the first phase of growth requires you to reexamine your understanding in the following areas:

Child development. As you learn new content, you learn about child development, as well as specific learning pathways for developmental areas such as language or social-emotional development. You may learn about research or theories on interactions between the new content and these developmental areas. You may also learn about particular curricula or assessment tools.

Standards. You learn about the guidelines undergirding your work. Most efforts to change or improve instructional practice have links to research and standards. Standards such as state early learning standards, provincial early learning frameworks, teacher core competency standards, Head Start performance standards, the Head Start Early Learning Outcomes Framework, and the Common Core State Standards provide a framework to guide teaching and learning. Research on how and what young children should be learning continually informs these standards and teacher learning. As part of your learning, you engage the research and standards and wrestle with how they relate to the children in your classroom.

Teaching practices. You learn new ways to observe and assess or learn new techniques that address individual learning needs. Application and practice form a vital counterpart to theory. If you begin the practice as soon as you learn the new content, the theory will become more real.

Policies and procedures. Instructional change affects policies and procedures. These effects can range from new assessment forms to new staff positions such as coaches or home visitors to new schedules and program routines. (For example, Renee is learning about the CLASS instrument, including descriptions of certain types of teacher-child interactions, and how to use this tool to improve her teaching practice. Kue now has a coach, which is a new position in his program. Kue is expected to meet regularly with his coach, and he is still learning what he should expect from the coach and what the coach expects from him during those meetings.)

You may sigh in discouragement when you have to learn a new policy or procedure at work. It takes time. Doing things differently, or adding something new, can disrupt daily routines and schedules until the new policy or procedure is integrated into practice and becomes routine. Fortunately, you'll often find that once established, new policies and procedures make things better, bring new information, and may even make life easier. One teacher commented at the end of a three-year initiative, "At first I thought it would mean more paperwork, but teaching has actually become easier and less stressful. If I need something for math, the information and ideas are directly in front of me."

You can see how learning about yourself and learning about content and strategy interact. The content knowledge you gain about how children learn, what they learn, and how you can promote their learning supports your sense of yourself as an effective teacher.

Guiding Questions: Learning About Content and Strategies

Here are some guiding questions to help you learn about content and strategies as you embark on change in your teaching:

> What content are you expected to learn? Is it theory, research, or practice? Is it about *how* children learn or about *what* they learn? Is it about teaching strategies? Is it about new policies or procedures?

> What do you think you already know about this?

> What do you already do that is related to this new content?

> What supports do you have in learning this content?

> What does your program expect of you in terms of applying this content? What high stakes may be involved?

> **If these questions raise concerns, try to find ways to address them:**
>
> › If you feel you are asked to learn a lot, try to break the learning into stages or steps, just as you would with children. Be patient and give yourself time.
>
> › If you know someone who already knows what you need to learn, or who seems comfortable with the new content, see if she is willing to act as a mentor or a learning partner. If she will let you, visit her classroom and watch her in action. Invite her to come and visit your classroom, too.
>
> › If you are not sure what supports you will have or what the organizational expectations are regarding your learning and applying the new content, have a conversation with your supervisor to gather more information.

To delve more deeply into your own understanding of cognitive learning, see the reproducible form titled "Piecing Together Cognitive Dimensions of Learning" on pages 79–80. This form will help you examine factors that influence how you take in new content knowledge. These factors, in turn, are affected by what is going on in your life.

Learning Through Interacting with Others

This dimension of learning is about relationships, or the people with whom you are learning. For teachers, this means learning from interactions with children, coworkers, families, and others in your classroom and program.

As Renee reflects on her relationships, she thinks about the children in her group. She wonders how to introduce more extended conversations with the dual language learners in her classroom. She wants to include her two assistant teachers as she learns to conduct these kinds of conversations with children. She also wonders how to share this strategy with families at conferences.

Kue is excited to work with a classroom coach and welcomes the opportunity to exchange ideas with other teachers. He is curious to see how the children will respond to some of the new strategies he is learning.

When Isobel thinks about her school's new social-emotional curriculum, she feels there will be no change for her children, as she is already doing the same thing with them every day. She wonders how her assistant teacher will respond to the training. Isobel wants to collaborate with the assistant teacher, and she hopes he doesn't cause confusion by trying to change classroom routines on his own.

Interacting with Children

As you begin to apply new content and strategies, you learn from the individual and collective responses of children in your classroom. As one teacher told us, "I learned by observing the experience of each child."

Observations like this may change teacher expectations about children's skills and knowledge. For example, when a teacher attended a conference workshop on using ramps and marbles to teach math and science concepts, the presenter showed a video where children used the ramps to create pathways for balls. The teacher was excited by this, and noted how the video changed her thinking about what young children can do. "The example of the ramps and the different things children could do with the ramps really stood out to me," she said. "Before, I thought, 'There's only so much you can do with a ramp.' But the kids in the video did quite a bit. I was amazed that children so young could do that."

How the children in your class function as a group also influences what you will learn. Perhaps you work with two groups of children each day—one group in a morning session and a different group of children in the afternoon. The two groups may have noticeably different dynamics, due to their unique ranges of developmental

You will learn a variety of effective teaching strategies based on your interactions with the children in your classroom. You may make changes in:

- the type of language you use (for example, using more math vocabulary words, such as *more*, *less*, *amount*, and *pattern*)

- the way you converse (for example, planning open-ended questions to invite longer conversations)

- how children relate to their environment (for example, having them create classroom labels for favorite learning centers instead of making labels yourself)

- how you conduct daily routines (for example, pulling math into the question of the day that greets parents and children) skills, knowledge, activity levels, English language skills, and ages. These different dynamics mean you have to adapt a new strategy to fit each group. For example, one teacher's morning class of four- and five-year-olds may enjoy reading and discussing a picture book in a large group and may easily recall details from previous readings. In the afternoon, with a group that includes three-year-olds, reading aloud to the whole group may not be as effective. Reading in small groups of two to three children and using stories with less text and more concrete ideas may work better.

Interacting with Adults

Changes in instructional practices usually affect the other adults in your classroom as well as the children. Some ways that adult interactions in the classroom might change are:

> **Lesson plans.** You may need more time for group lesson planning as you incorporate new ideas, strategies, or routines.

> **Roles.** The roles of the adults in your classroom may change. For example, you may each start working with small groups of students to build skills.

> **Partners.** New people may partner with you. For example, you may be assigned a coach, or you may be asked to mentor others.

Like many teachers, you may work with other staff in the classroom. Sometimes all the adults in the classroom can attend professional development together, which helps the teaching team establish a common core of knowledge. One teacher put it succinctly, "Having assistants attend training so we are all on the same page supported children's growth. They could help plan." When coworkers and colleagues are all making changes together, the group can provide mutual support, valuable feedback, and new ideas for one another. A group may help generate solutions to challenges or problems that arise as you carry out changes in practice or procedures.

Interacting with Coaches and Mentors

Coaches, mentors, supervisors, and others who partner with you in your professional development move your growth forward. Like coworkers, they may bring fresh perspectives, along with their own experience and knowledge, to the learning partnership. They may help you recognize your own expertise. They can build your confidence, too, as one teacher noted: "The math coach comes in and says, 'You can do this, but you don't realize you already do some of this.'" Coaches and mentors build on your strengths by scaffolding new concepts onto existing instructional knowledge and practice.

Having solid, reliable relationships with your colleagues can help anchor you as you enter the unknown, making it easier to take risks. You become part of a learning community. When given the chance to exchange ideas or observe one another, teachers learn from each other. It is usually easier to institute change in your own behavior when others around you are doing the same.

Interacting with the Work Environment

Each organization and school has structures, policies, procedures, and an informal culture that affect how things are done. For instance, while some programs seldom use small groups as learning experiences, others provide small-group learning as a regular part of their curriculum. If you are not familiar with small-group learning, you may need more support from your coach or supervisor to try it. Because of complicated pay structures and job definitions in public school classrooms, only the teachers (not the paraprofessionals) attend workshops and other professional development opportunities. This means that not all the adults in the classroom hear the same information about instructional changes or new teaching practices. When paraprofessionals or assistant teachers are not included in the same training as the teachers, teachers in these settings may need to find other ways to involve the paraprofessionals in the instructional change efforts.

Community context affects children and their families as well as teachers and their workplaces. You can understand and experience the daily lives of children and families by living in the community, having conversations with parents and colleagues, conducting home visits, shopping in the community, and attending community events. You can then link your understanding of the unique strengths and challenges of the community into your daily teaching practice.

Guiding Questions: Learning Through Interacting with Others

Here are some guiding questions to help you learn through interacting with others as you embark on change in your teaching:

> How will this change affect your interactions with the children in your classroom?

> How will this change affect your interactions with coworkers in your classroom (who may be people you supervise or who supervise you)?

> Have you and your fellow teachers established a shared set of knowledge about the new effort? If not, how can you share that information?

> How does your context (the way you do things in your program or in your community) influence how you do your work?

> What do you know about the community context of children in your classroom? How could you find out more? How do you apply that to your teaching?

If these questions raise concerns, find ways to address them:

> Set aside regular time for your teaching team to discuss the new content or strategies and how you are carrying out this change in the classroom.

> Learn about the surrounding community and program. Your supervisor and coworkers can be resources for learning. The best way to know more about children is by establishing relationships with their families.

As a teacher, you face a complex task: integrating new content and strategies, managing your own responses, and changing your interactions with others. You may express resistance to new ideas because you know change is not simple: that learning one new strategy or activity leads to further questions. For instance, earlier we suggested an example of changing your classroom labeling system so the children in your classroom create the labels. This idea initially came from a training session on print awareness. The trainer asked the teaching staff to think about how they used labels in their classrooms and about who used the different labels in their classrooms.

This led to an ongoing discussion among all the teaching staff about what labels they used in their classrooms and about the purposes of various labels. One teacher was proud of the beautiful signs labeling each learning center in her classroom. She had taken tremendous care to make them clear and lovely to look at, with pictures to match. Over the years other teachers had admired and copied her example. After the training on print awareness and subsequent discussions about labels—in particular, which labels are actually used by children—she decided to take down the learning center signs. She had conversations at group time with the children in her classroom about each learning center and how it was used. She then asked the children to make a new sign for each learning center, helping them with spelling when asked. She shared this story with other teachers in her learning community.

The complexities of teaching are part of what makes teaching rewarding. What you learn in one area you can apply in other areas as well. For instance, teachers grow in their overall use of assessment when asked to plan and set goals for children based on assessment data. One teacher observed, "I see now how I can be more technical. My coteacher created a developmental chart; we check off the skills and note how well the children grasp each concept—not just at year-end but how they are progressing throughout the year."

How Does This Phase of Growth Affect Your Daily Practice?

Making changes in your practice as a teacher influences almost every aspect of your work. Your daily routines, groups, environment, and lesson plans may undergo profound ups and downs as you integrate new material and practices. Each phase in the three-phase growth cycle may bring up different issues, and it is helpful to explore what you may go through. In this chapter and the next two chapters, we look at how change impacts:

▶ your professional identity

▶ dilemmas you encounter

▶ feelings you experience

As you reflect on your work as a teacher, you may recognize these concepts, feelings, and dilemmas from your daily experiences.

Your Professional Identity: Who You Are as a Teacher

As a result of traveling through the three phases of growth—learning, practicing, and sharing and modeling—you may find yourself thinking about your identity as a teacher in a new light. Researchers Clandinin and Connelly have investigated how teachers understand their professional practice. Clandinin and Connelly write about teaching as a narrative, or a story teachers develop through their experiences.[4] Think of your professional identity as a story you are creating. Your story as a teacher illuminates your practice, beliefs, and values.[5] That story forms a picture of how you see yourself as a teacher, how effective you feel, how you define your style of teaching, and what you see as your strengths and weaknesses in the classroom. It is also the story of how you take what you know about learning and teaching and bring it to life in your own way.

So when change comes to your classroom, it is likely to have an impact on how you see yourself as a teacher, because it changes your story. Your professional identity may alter as you are introduced to new knowledge, new strategies, new experiences, and sometimes even new values or beliefs about teaching and learning. To see how the smaller events of your daily life as a teacher contribute to your larger story as a teacher, use the reproducible form on pages 81–82, "Short Story of My Teaching."

Encountering Dilemmas: What and How You Practice

When you encounter change that aligns with your current beliefs and classroom practices, it fits easily with your story of how and why you teach. This type of change is easy to integrate because it seems to flow with what you already do, think, and feel. However, new initiatives often present dilemmas for teachers.

Learning from Dilemmas

Dilemmas require you to reflect on your own values, take different perspectives, think creatively and logically, and make conscious choices. Wrestling with dilemmas is a rich opportunity to become more conscious of your values and priorities about teaching.

A dilemma arises when you have to choose between two competing or contradictory ideas. Sometimes a dilemma arises because some part of a new initiative conflicts with your existing core beliefs or values. For example, when teachers first learn about how to teach early literacy, they often express concern that focusing on literacy will detract from their primary teaching focus on children's social-emotional development. This concern reflects competing beliefs or values: an emphasis on academic skills versus an emphasis on social-emotional development.

Sometimes dilemmas arise from competing priorities. For example, one program asked teachers to learn and use a new online assessment system. The teachers were expected to gather assessment documentation on thirty to forty different skills by observing children interacting in the classroom at least three times each year. During the first year of using the new assessment tool, teachers often complained that they felt caught between spending extended time observing students to gather adequate assessment documentation and actually teaching the children.

> Wrestling with dilemmas is a rich opportunity to become more conscious of your values and priorities about teaching.

Understanding a dilemma is the first step in coming to terms with it. Identify what seems to be in conflict. Here are some questions to help you examine the dilemma more closely:

- What do you believe about children and learning in this area? How does that seem to fit, or not fit, with this new initiative?

- Is something bothering you about how this change affects teaching, learning, teachers, children, or families? What is it?

- What questions do you have about the idea that seems to be in conflict with your beliefs or values?

- Do you feel torn between different priorities? If so, what are the two priorities that seem to be in conflict?

▶ What resources might help you learn more about each of these priorities?

▶ Who could be a helpful ally in wrestling with this dilemma?

▶ What are your options?

▶ What are the potential consequences of each option?

You may find yourself temporarily stalled, unable to move ahead or to come to a resolution. Feeling stuck is part of the process of resolving a dilemma. If you find yourself stuck, be aware of what your questions or tough issues are, and remember to give yourself time. You may need additional time, more information, new experiences, or new perspectives before you can successfully resolve a complex dilemma.

Both-And Thinking

Another way to approach a dilemma is to ask yourself if you can embrace both options, rather than choosing one or the other. This requires looking very carefully at each of the options to see if you can integrate them.

Sometimes dilemmas are dilemmas only in our own minds. They may not *need* to be dilemmas. Either-or thinking can sometimes get in the way of moving forward. For example, teachers of young children often question whether they should use a play-based curriculum or a more academic curriculum. The field as a whole is emphasizing academic skills such as literacy and math more than it used to, and many teachers are afraid this emphasis will push out the existing emphasis on play. If teachers use either-or thinking, they assume that the options are incompatible with each other. They end up fighting the changes or being resentful and worried about harming the children. If teachers take a both-and approach, they

Once you identify your dilemma, do not ignore it. It is not likely to go away on its own, and it can bring additional stress and distraction to your daily work. Try to see your dilemma as a chance to better understand and articulate what you do and why you do it. Once you have a good understanding of your dilemma, come to terms with it. Coming to terms with teaching dilemmas may mean:

- resolving the conflict between the two ideas

- acclimating to a new idea

- choosing one option over the other

- deciding to live with the dissonance between the two ideas

- sticking with what you know best

assume instead that the options can work together, and they embrace both. They understand that children need instruction that's both playful *and* hands-on in order to learn new material. They realize they don't have to push out play. They understand it is essential to integrate play in both child-directed and teacher-directed times.

The following thought bubbles illustrate how both-and thinking can lead to a more balanced approach in your teaching. Meanwhile, either-or thinking may narrow choices and opportunities for both you and the children. Think of your end goal as you weigh the two sides of any dilemma.

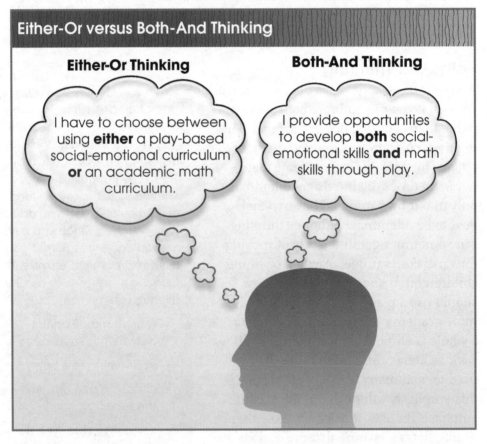

Either-Or versus Both-And Thinking

Either-Or Thinking

I have to choose between using **either** a play-based social-emotional curriculum **or** an academic math curriculum.

Both-And Thinking

I provide opportunities to develop **both** social-emotional skills **and** math skills through play.

As teachers go through this first phase of growth, Teachers Learn, they often share similar dilemmas or challenges. The dilemmas teachers face are unique to their particular background and setting, but they all seem to fall into three categories:

- risky change
- not enough time
- too many changes

Risky Change

The biggest challenge of entering into change is giving up the comfort of the familiar in hope that the stress of change will be outweighed by the positive impact. You are motivated to change your practice by the hope or belief that children will benefit. However, you cannot know what the impact of a change will be—no matter what research, books, workshop speakers, families, or colleagues tell you—until you experience it yourself in your own classroom. Because of this, it is not unusual to feel a little stuck in this first phase. You want to go forward, but you also feel that the change is risky.

The more you can learn about the changes ahead, including the potential impact of those changes, the better prepared you will be to move forward. It is also helpful to seek out support as you enter into unknown territory. Talk to colleagues, mentors, family, and friends during the process of change.

Not Enough Time

A second big challenge of change is the allocation of time. Instructional change demands additional time in terms of learning, planning, and implementation. These time demands can make it difficult for you to do your job in other areas. You may worry you are spending too much time in the classroom focused on new content and strategies you are learning at the expense of other learning and development. Or change may affect the time you spend out of the classroom, making you feel unable to meet administrative demands such as completing reporting forms or lesson plans.

To deal with demands on your time, prioritize with colleagues and get additional supports if possible. For example, some teachers join a peer study group or ask for work time to reflect and plan with colleagues. Most importantly, be patient with yourself. You know that when children are working on a new skill, they often focus their activities on the practicing of that skill until they have reached competence. Allow yourself the same time to learn. Remember that, like the children in your classroom, you will eventually integrate your new knowledge and skills into a balanced approach to learning and teaching.

Too Many Changes

A third challenge of change is feeling overwhelmed by too many changes at one time. For instance, your program may have entered into several different professional development initiatives at once. Or perhaps your program is entering into a new partnership to combine special education and preschool classrooms while bringing on a new curriculum.

If you are feeling overwhelmed by the amount of change happening, you may need to bring your concerns to your supervisor. Your supervisor may be able to help you by shifting priorities so you can take new steps one at a time. For example, your program might institute the new curriculum for a year or so before switching assessment systems. You may also have the option to give up some responsibilities that no longer make sense or redistribute tasks so all teachers maintain a balanced workload.

Dealing with Feelings

Many teachers express anxiety as they embark on instructional change. This is especially true in the Teachers Learn phase. Researchers Victoria Marsick and Karen Watkins note that because teachers have worked hard to become good teachers, they feel more vulnerable when they're asked to unlearn past lessons and try new ones.[6] When what you thought you knew is called into question, you may feel as if coworkers and supervisors are scrutinizing your teaching identity and practice with children. You may suddenly feel less confident or competent as you explore unfamiliar teaching territory. Although it can be difficult to admit your feelings of vulnerability, doing so can help you recognize your emotional responses to the new demands. If you share your feelings with others, you may be surprised to find they are feeling exactly the same way.

It can be overwhelming to learn something new. It is important to be aware of your feelings. Here are feelings we have heard teachers express during this phase of growth:

Anxiety. You may become anxious when you aren't sure what comes next. It's hard to stay focused on the here and now, taking one step at a time. Instead, you become consumed with what-ifs. You ask, "What if the children don't like the activities? What if the children in my class don't make progress? What if I am a total mess when observers visit?" Following are some of the specific fears you may feel:

❱ being unable to learn the content

❱ teaching the activities incorrectly

❱ children not responding to the activities

❱ harming children by asking them to do activities they aren't ready for

Confusion. When you are learning new material and content, you may find it is easy to get confused. You may not remember the steps of the game you are trying to teach. You may walk out of a training feeling confident, but when you try to explain the information to your team, you just can't find the words. Learning new words, concepts, and developmental pathways does not happen overnight. Growth means taking a few steps forward, then backward, then forward again.

Resentment. You may resent being asked to change how you organize your lessons, schedule your day, or set up your environment. You may want to hang onto the comfortable, familiar ways you have used in the past. You may be offended by the suggestion that your methods are somehow lacking.

Frustration. You may feel frustrated by a suggested change. You can't figure out how it fits with your philosophy or how to implement the strategy. As one teacher said, "The first year I was frustrated because I thought maybe the new math initiative was not age appropriate. I always think about children's social-emotional development; I didn't want the children to be frustrated because they didn't get it."

Hesitation. You may feel unsure what to do as you start to introduce new strategies. As one teacher said, "I felt hesitant: unfamiliar with the subject and how difficult it was to teach. I wasn't familiar with the concepts and terms."

Reflecting on your emotional responses to change—whatever those feelings may be—can be a powerful tool for adult learners. It can help you understand how your feelings affect your own learning and can inform your interactions with children in the classroom. Take some time to reflect on your emotional responses to a change you currently face in your teaching by using the reproducible form "Challenges and Overcoming Obstacles" on pages 83–84.

Chances are, you feel more than one emotion about the change. You may even feel conflicting emotions. For example, you may feel both excited about learning new strategies and anxious about trying them in the classroom. Most teachers have mixed feelings about new challenges.

Naming hopes, fears, and burning questions is a strategy we have used to help teachers recognize and balance their feelings at the beginning of a change. Use the reproducible form titled "Hopes, Fears, and Burning Questions" on pages 85–86 to explore your reactions and feelings.

Here are a few final suggestions to help you as you go through the first phase of growth, Teachers Learn:

- Give it time. Be patient with yourself and others.

- Practice, by yourself and with others.

- Make sure you understand your role.

- Make sure you have the tools you need.

- Find a learning partner: a critical friend, mentor, or coach.

- Work with others to make adjustments if needed.

- If possible, participate in planning the new process and evaluating how it is working.

- If possible, give up another procedure that no longer needs doing.

- Admit your feelings and share them with others.

The next chapter will investigate the second phase of growth, Teachers Practice. This phase links what you learn to what you do.

References

1. Karen M. LaParo, Robert C. Pianta, and Megan Stuhlman,"The Classroom Assessment Scoring System: Findings from the Prekindergarten Year," *The Elementary School Journal* 104, no. 5 (2004): 409–426.

2. Sarah V. Mackenzie and George Marnik, "Maine Program Helps Teachers Learn from That Voice: Inner Voice Tells Teachers How to Grow," *Journal of Staff Development* 25, no. 3 (Summer 2004): 50–57.

3. Lilian G. Katz, "Developmental Stages of Preschool Teachers," *Elementary School Journal* 73, no. 1 (1972): 50–54.

4. F. Michael Connelly and D. Jean Clandinin, "Personal Practical Knowledge and the Modes of Knowing: Relevance for Teaching and Learning," in *Learning and Teaching the Ways of Knowing*, ed. Elliot Eisner (Chicago: University of Chicago Press, 1985): 184.

5. Douwe Beijaard, Paulien C. Meijer, and Nico Verloop, "Reconsidering Research on Teachers' Professional Identity," *Teaching and Teacher Education* 20 (2004): 107–128.

6. Victoria J. Marsick and Karen E. Watkins, "Continuous Learning in the Workplace," *Adult Learning* 3, no. 4 (1992): 9–12.

Piecing Together Cognitive Dimensions of Learning

Many factors affect how you, as an adult learner, take in new knowledge. These factors, in turn, may be affected by what is going on in your life at the time. Answer the following questions to help you identify these factors.

Think about a new area of content that you are learning or want to learn.

What's going on in your life that may affect your ability to learn at this time?

What content do you already know?

What opportunities do you have to practice and then process what you have learned?

What opportunities do you have for feedback and problem solving (coaching, mentoring, reflective supervision) as you apply the new content?

In the puzzle pieces below, write down as many ideas as you can that may help you gain the knowledge, confidence, skills, strategies, and competence you will need to excel in the new content area.

Short Story of My Teaching

Think about a particular time period during a typical day of teaching. It might be morning arrivals, circle time, outdoor time, or mealtime. Replay that time in your head as if you were watching yourself.

Take a few minutes to write down your recollection.

When you are done writing, think about each of the following questions.

How were you feeling about your teaching during this time? Have your feelings changed? If so, how have they changed?

If you had to describe what kind of teacher you were during this story, what words would you use?

Does your story have a conflict or crisis? If so, what is it? How was it resolved?

If you could rewind this situation like a movie and start over, what would you change or keep the same? Why?

Challenges and Overcoming Obstacles

Describe a challenge you are currently experiencing.

Write down what is challenging about the situation.

Review your answers to the questions above. Be aware of the feelings that arise as you reflect on the challenge you identified. **Check the feelings below that apply to you. Feel free to add feelings not already listed.**

☐ Anger
☐ Anticipation
☐ Anxiety
☐ Confidence
☐ Confusion
☐ Curiosity
☐ Cynicism
☐ Doubt

☐ Excitement
☐ Fear
☐ Hope
☐ Resignation
☐ _____
☐ _____
☐ _____

➡️

Review your list of feelings. Do your reactions seem mostly positive or mostly negative? Explain.

How have you navigated similar feelings or situations in the past? Write down at least three strategies or resources you have used.

How might you use your past experience with similar feelings to deal with your current challenge?

Hopes, Fears, and Burning Questions

Think about a change you are facing. Describe it here:

Complete the following items with your selected change in mind.

 Describe your **HOPES** for the children, for your classroom, for your program, or for yourself.

 Write down your **FEARS** for the children, for your classroom, for your program, or for yourself.

 Write down at least three **BURNING QUESTIONS** you have about your identified change.

Now review your burning questions. Sort your questions by putting symbols next to each. Then address your questions by following the suggestions in boldface.

This symbol [?] indicates a question that a friend or colleague can help you answer. **Whom can you seek out?**

This symbol (✓) indicates a question that will require more time to resolve. **Set up a time frame for yourself.**

This symbol ▭ indicates a question that would benefit from additional professional development or further study. **List options for classes or additional learning.**

Now think about a new strategy or resource you are willing to explore to face your current challenge, and write it down here.

It is important to use your go-to strategies *and* to push yourself to try new strategies. This will help you learn and grow professionally and personally.

5 TEACHERS PRACTICE

Awan worked hard for several months to help her students notice rhymes in the stories she read aloud. She used a technique she'd learned in a literacy workshop called a cloze procedure: she omitted the final words of familiar rhymes, such as "Five little ducks went out to play, over the hills and far _(away)_ ," encouraging her students to supply the missing words. She played rhyming games with children's names during circle time.

When her literacy mentor shared assessment results with her, Awan saw that her efforts seemed to be paying off with most of the four-year-olds in her classroom. Many children recognized rhyming words and many could produce rhymes. Quite a few dual language learners appeared to be catching on, but she noticed that several of the Hmong children who were dual language learners still did not seem to understand the concept of a rhyme. She and her mentor talked about this and decided to look into some other strategies. Her mentor agreed to observe some of the planned rhyming activities and give Awan her feedback. Awan also talked about the situation with other teachers at her site.

At the suggestion of her mentor and colleagues, one day at lunch, Awan began playfully making rhymes using the different foods at her table, such as "pears and chairs," "bread and head," and "peas and knees." This game made the children giggle, and two girls began playing it with her. Then they started making up rhymes for other objects around them. Awan could hardly contain her excitement: these girls were two of the Hmong children she had been concerned about. The next day, she played the same game at lunch. More children joined in, and she noticed many of the Hmong children seemed to be participating. She played the lunchtime rhyme game with children all week. Before long, she noticed some of the Hmong girls playing the rhyme game in the classroom without her as they entered the dramatic play area. Awan smiled to herself as she realized she had added one more strategy to her early literacy toolbox.

In Chapter 4, you considered what you learn during the first phase of instructional change: Teachers Learn. In this chapter, you will delve into the second phase of growth: Teachers Practice. In this phase, the rubber meets the road as you apply what you learn.

You may find that practice provides an opportunity to deepen your own learning as a teacher. Like Awan in the example that opens this chapter, you learn from children's responses, from your own and others' observations, and from formal and informal assessments. You learn from family communications about what children do at home. You learn from other teachers, who bring their own teaching styles and adaptations to strategies and interactions. As you dig deeper, you may run into challenges, learning as much from failure as from success. Practice is an opportunity for you as a teacher to take ownership of your own learning.

What You Practice

Let's view the practice phase of growth through the lenses of the three dimensions of learning: learning about yourself, learning about content and strategies, and learning through interacting with others. (See page 57 for more on these dimensions.) In the second phase, you shift your focus from yourself to others. In other words, in the first phase you ask yourself, "What am I learning? What does that mean for my approach to teaching?" In the second phase you ask yourself, "What do I do with what I learn? What happens when I do it?" Once you begin to learn new content and strategies, you apply the new knowledge in your classroom, with families, and in your program. You begin to find out what works and what doesn't work. You expand your professional identity and relationships.

Adjusting Your Professional Identity

This dimension of learning can be both exciting and a little scary during the practice phase. It is exciting because during this phase, you integrate what you have learned into your teaching identity and your classroom. Remember your teaching story in Chapter 4? As you take ownership of new strategies, you add to your story. Training, research, and coaching give you knowledge; you make it your own through practice.

This dimension of learning is also scary, because owning your learning—using it with understanding—is not necessarily easy. As you put new knowledge into action, your learning process can get complicated. Awan's story at the beginning of this chapter is a good example of the deeper exploration that occurs through practice. Awan practiced the strategies she had learned, and she succeeded with many children. However, when she and her mentor looked more closely, Awan realized she had not accomplished her goal of reaching all the children. Awan wasn't sure how to proceed. She could have continued what she was doing, hoping more children would eventually catch on. But instead, she decided to look more closely at the challenge before her. She wondered if the Hmong children in her class needed more than just time, due to language barriers. She wondered if these children needed different strategies, too. Awan sought out more information and kept practicing, trying different strategies in hopes of learning more from children's responses.

> Training, research, and coaching give you knowledge; you make it your own through practice.

As you practice new strategies, you may lose some of the sense of predictability and control you have felt in the classroom in the past. Developmental psychologist Jean Piaget developed a concept he called "disequilibrium" to explain how new knowledge transforms our thinking.[1] According to Piaget, we all have a set of ideas in our mind that explains our world and how it works. For teachers, that set of ideas includes ideas about how children learn and about the most important teaching practices. When a new idea or observation comes forward, especially one that is unexpected or doesn't fit well with our existing ideas, we feel uncomfortable or off-balance. We want to find the balance, or equilibrium, again. This makes us question our previous assumptions, and we either layer the new information onto our existing ideas or transform our thinking to incorporate the new idea. This cognitive conflict and its resulting mental reorganization leads to new or more accurate thinking.[2] In other words: as you put new learning into action, you may run into surprising results that raise new questions about what you thought you knew.

This disequilibrium may affect your professional identity. As a teacher, you may move in and out of feeling competent. One teacher described this phenomenon as follows: "After my first year, I had an inflated idea of my ability. I thought, 'I have math under control.' I recently became more aware of the needs of individual children in the large group. I am still working it out."

In the first phase of growth, Teachers Learn, you may entertain doubts about new methods and the theories behind them. The second phase of growth, Teachers Practice, presents an opportunity to address those doubts by investigating how a strategy plays out in reality. When something unexpected, contradictory, or puzzling happens in your classroom, you ask questions to find out more. As you ask questions about new teaching content or methods, you begin to understand more about how children learn and about effective teaching methods. Through practice, you learn what is effective, what doesn't work, and what needs to be adapted to make it succeed with the children in your classroom. You integrate new learning into your existing knowledge and methods.

> Be flexible and patient with your own learning during the practice phase.

When you see children thrive, it takes away your fears. One teacher noted: "I was surprised to see how much kids can learn. It increased my comfort. The children were excited and enthusiastic. . . . We saw three-year-olds who could extend patterns because we tried it. Even if they didn't learn it now, when they get to the older classroom, they will catch on."

Even though you can learn much from your mistakes, trial and error can be frustrating. And feeling off-balance, that sense of disequilibrium, is by definition uncomfortable. So this dimension of practice may be challenging in terms of your professional identity. You may struggle with feelings of incompetence and uncertainty. What is more, practice doesn't happen in a vacuum. When you practice as a teacher, you do so before an audience of children, coworkers, families, and supervisors. At times, you may be your own harshest critic. You may get discouraged. It's important to be flexible and patient with your own learning during the practice phase. You know that persistence is key to successful learning for children, and the same is true for you as a teacher.

> **Guiding Questions:** **Adjusting Your Professional Identity**
>
> **As you practice new strategies and adjust your professional identity, here are some questions to ponder:**
>
> › How do you think that went? Did things go the way you expected?
>
> › How did you feel while you were doing it? How do you feel about it now?
>
> › Did anything surprise you? If so, what was it? Why did it surprise you?
>
> › What did you like or dislike about the experience?
>
> › What did you notice about your own teaching as you did this?
>
> › What additional supports, tools, or resources might help you?
>
> › What have you learned about your teaching practice from trying this?
>
> **If these questions raise concerns for you, think about ways to address your concerns:**
>
> › Think about what you would like to change in your strategy. Given the children's responses, do you need to adapt the way you do the activity or the materials you use?
>
> › Talk with another teacher or early childhood professional about your strategy. Listen to your colleague's suggestions and decide if they would help you.
>
> › Remember, things seldom go smoothly the first time we try them. Give yourself and children time to get used to a new strategy before judging how it is working.
>
> › Plan your next strategy with your observations and children's responses in mind.

Practicing Content and Strategies

Practicing new content and strategies gives you an opportunity to increase your understanding of how young children learn. As you try out different strategies and see what does and doesn't work, new questions often arise.

As Piagetian scholar Dr. George Forman points out, "Experience is not the best teacher. One must reflect on experience in order to learn."[3]

The skills of observation and documentation will help you reflect on what happens when you apply new learning. You will also need time to reflect on what you observe, to interpret what you think it means, and to figure out how you will use that information. Educator Terry Borton's "What? So What? Now What?" model describes a cycle of questions you can use to learn and grow continuously.[4] "What?" refers to what you have learned. "So What?" is about applying what you have learned and making meaning from that application. "Now What?" refers to what you choose to do next with what you've learned. Then you cycle back to "What?"—which may be new or revised.

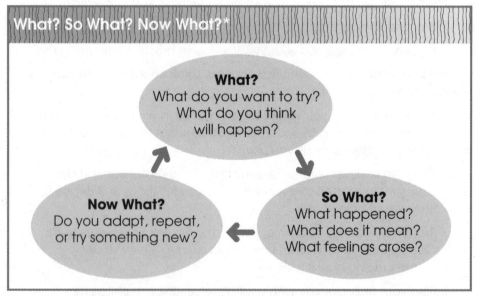

*The "What? So What? Now What?" model is from Terry Borton. *Reach, Touch, and Teach: Student Concerns and Process Education* (New York: McGraw-Hill, 1970). Used with permission of McGraw-Hill Education.

The "what" that you are learning and practicing might be:

- new curriculum
- new instructional strategies
- new routines or schedules
- new learning environments
- new assessment processes
- new standards

To determine your "so what," or to evaluate the impact of your new knowledge and strategy, you might use the following tools:

Direct student assessment. If you are fortunate, your program or professional development initiative offers an assessment tool designed specifically to assess the impact of your efforts on your students. If not, you may have to design your own direct student assessment tools. Simple checklists and anecdotal records can help you measure your students' progress.

Observation and documentation. Choose a time of day you want to observe, and take some notes. These days it's easy to make video recordings in the classroom, once you have the appropriate permissions. If you want to see yourself in action, ask a colleague to take a quick video. It doesn't have to be perfect to give you an idea of how things went. Then you can observe yourself teaching and think about what worked, what didn't work, and what you want to do about it.

Journaling or writing down the story of the day, or the story of a segment of the day. It may be particularly helpful to write about days or experiences that stand out for you. They might stand out because they were unusual, because you felt things went either really well or really badly, or because something surprising occurred.

Asking yourself, "How did it go?" at the end of the day. This is a very informal formative assessment that you can easily and naturally build into your ride home or into an informal conversation with your teaching team. If you ask yourself, "How did it go?" and you answer, "Not so great," you can start thinking about what you may want to do differently next time or start adjusting your plans for the next day. It is easy to miss what went well each day. It is important to think about that, too, so you can more consciously replicate the good stuff.

Regardless of how you gather information, once you have collected it, then it's time to think about what it means. This is where you really think about your "so what," or interpret what you have observed. You must study the effect of your actions on learning and ask, "What was the result for children or families, and how do I know?" Here are some things to keep in mind as you think about your "so what":

▸ What specifically were you trying to do?

▸ What did you expect or hope would happen?

▶ What did happen? How do you know?

▶ If things didn't go as expected, why do you think that is?

▶ Do you need more information before you can interpret the effects of your efforts?

▶ What new questions do you have?

Once you have spent time thinking about the "so what," it's time to move on to the "now what." This may mean setting new goals based on observations or assessment data. It may mean you make adjustments or additions to a strategy and try it again. It may mean you ask more questions or gather more information. Or it may mean you try again because you need more practice to develop comfort, you need more time to establish a routine with children, or you saw positive results that you hope to repeat.

As you try out new techniques in the classroom, you may repeat this "What? So What? Now What?" cycle several times, gathering more information, making additional adjustments, and continuing to look at impact as you fine-tune a strategy. The following story illustrates this ongoing process.

Casey, a preschool teacher, experienced the cycle many times while supporting children's math skills and understanding. Casey explained, "As a teacher, I was working really hard to help my preschoolers learn and practice their early math skills. I went to a workshop on using grid games to teach math. The children loved the games, and most of them improved their skills. When we started playing the games, many children counted by just grabbing some items or using one-to-one correspondence. After playing the games with children for several weeks, I saw many children counting correctly without having to match one-to-one with the dots on the dice. I saw children counting in other activities throughout the classroom. Several of the kindergarten-bound children were able to count ten to twenty objects quickly and accurately."

Casey continued, "But there was one kindergarten-bound child who didn't make progress, no matter what I did. I gave him special help, and we worked on counting small sets of objects. Sometimes when we worked together, he would be able to count ten objects accurately. We celebrated, I would give him a sticker, and the next day, he wouldn't even remember to start with the number one when he counted. I panicked when I was unable to help him. I didn't know what to do and felt like a failure.

"Thankfully, a few weeks later, I attended a math training led by educator Brian Mowry and learned that children who are having difficulty remembering how to count objects are operating from their amygdala, a more primitive part of the brain.[5] Brian told us we needed to give children experiences to help them develop the frontal lobe of their brains. This, he said, would help them improve their ability to retain what they are learning."

Casey explained, "Brian showed us how to create a counting tool for children who can count to two but are struggling to count further. The tool uses a shoelace, two clothespins, and Unifix Cubes. He instructed us to string three Unifix Cubes on the shoelace and secure the ends with the clothespins. To count the cubes, the teacher holds onto the clothespins and stretches the shoestring tight. The child holds the cube on his left and says, 'One, then locks it to the next cube and says, 'Two,' then locks the first two cubes to the third one and says, 'Three.' The child must use his own hands to lock the cubes together, because that makes his hands cross the midline and engage the frontal lobe of his brain to build his memory for counting.* Brian told us to also enlist family members and teach them how to use the cubes with their child. The counting cube set is sent home, and the family members practice with their child. When the child succeeds at home, the family sends the cube set back to school. The teacher checks the child's progress, and if the child succeeds, the teacher adds one more cube onto the shoestring, and so on. The shoestring can accommodate counting at least twenty cubes.

"This method was fabulous!" Casey exclaimed. "It was so exciting to see it work with the child I had been worried about. Once we tried it in the classroom and shared it with his mom, he began to count small numbers of objects accurately and consistently. Later, his mom and I were thrilled to watch him confidently count objects in a math game at our family carnival. This strategy was so successful that all the teachers in our center now use it. If a family is unable to follow through and support their child's success, we have agreed to assign an adult (such as the center director or assistant teacher) to the child to fill in for the family so that every child has a chance to grow and learn."[6]

This story beautifully illustrates the power of professional development paired with practice. If we analyze it using the "What? So What? Now What?" model, the "what" is using grid games to build counting skills. At first, Casey found success in using the grid game strategy exactly as she had learned it. She gathered information to discover "so what" by observing children's counting strategies as they played the games. She

---

*The midline is an invisible line separating the left side of the body from the right side. As a child develops movement patterns that cross the midline of the body, the brain builds and strengthens neural pathways that cross the midline of the brain. These pathways help the right and left halves of the brain communicate with each other. The more integrated the two halves are, the more quickly, flexibly, adaptably, and deeply the brain can think.

found when she looked more closely that the grid game strategy was not working as she had expected for every child. Informed by her observations, she determined that her "now what" was to adapt the strategy by playing the game individually and frequently with the child for whom the strategy had not been working well. Based on her knowledge about development of counting skills, she also limited the activities to counting a small number of objects. When her interactions and observations showed that this still didn't work, she had more questions. Why was this child able to count to ten at times, yet unable to retain counting skills from day to day? Was there another skill the child needed to work on in order to do this? Since the current strategy wasn't working, was there a way to adapt it further? Or did she need to look at a different strategy?

Casey knew from her education and experience in early childhood education, her math workshop, and her own observations that she needed more information in order to understand her observations. At another math training, she learned more about the impact of brain development on counting skills. She also learned a new related strategy that seemed promising to address her problem. She tried this new strategy *and* engaged the help of the child's mom, who also used the strategy at home with her child. Both Casey and the mom observed the child's reactions. Through persistence, exploration of a variety of strategies based on expanded knowledge of child development, and careful observation, they were able to help this child learn to count. In particular, Casey found herself stepping back to focus on a more basic skill that the child needed to develop before he could benefit from the grid games. Now Casey, her fellow teachers, and families at her center have a new strategy for teaching counting. In the process, Casey and her coworkers developed a larger framework for understanding and addressing children's development of counting skills.

Now that we have outlined the "What? So What? Now What?" process, turn to the reproducible form "Trying a New Strategy" on page 105 to complete your own plan for trying out a new teaching strategy.

As you practice new teaching approaches, you may encounter contradictions or puzzles. You must take in new information by either adapting what you know about learning and teaching or adding new concepts to your knowledge. One example of adaptation is something we learned from a workshop we presented on patterns. We described how preschool children generally begin to learn about patterns: first they identify a pattern, then they copy a pattern from a model, then they move to extending a pattern, and finally they create their own patterns. The teachers who attended our workshop began to do more patterning activities with children, and they observed children's reactions. Some teachers noted that they were seeing children who could extend a pattern before they could identify that it was a pattern. We shared these observations with all the teachers at every site, and we changed how we talked about pattern development. We still described the elements of understanding patterns as identifying, copying, extending, and creating, but we stopped saying that children understood these elements in a specific order. Instead, we encouraged teachers to observe children's responses in order to plan patterning experiences.

In this example, we began with an idea about the sequence of developing pattern understanding in preschool children. Then we experienced a contradiction or questioning of the sequence, based on direct experience with children. We decided to adapt our original idea, adding the idea that the steps may not happen in a specific order. Teachers' observations of children's responses may range from noting specific information on a learning area, such as understanding patterns, to observing broader child development, such as young children's movement in and out of demonstrating a skill until it is fully developed.

| Guiding Questions: | Practicing Content and Strategies |

As you learn new content and strategies, here are some questions to ponder:

> What did you notice about the response from children (or from families)?

> Did anything unexpected happen? How was it different from your expectations?

> How will you determine the impact of the new strategy?

> What worked? What didn't work? How do you know?

> Did you give it enough time?

> What do you want to repeat? What do you want to change?

> Do you need additional information or resources?

> **If these questions raise concerns for you, think about ways to address your concerns:**
>
> > Find ways to determine how effective your strategy was. Look at your goals, your observations, children's responses, children's engagement, and short developmental checklists based on expected skills.
>
> > Give a strategy time, then decide what changes you might make. Then try it again with those changes. Don't worry about repetition. Children need and love repetitive experiences to learn new material.

Getting and Using Feedback from Others

As a teacher, you depend on others to help you determine the impact of your new approaches. In the practice phase of growth, you apply new ideas with children or families, often in partnership with your colleagues. Responses from all these people help you fine-tune new methods and integrate new knowledge.

You can learn a lot from children's reactions to new strategies. Children's enthusiasm and interest are great motivators. When you experience this kind of success, you want to continue refining your new practices. Here are some examples of children's interest in new math learning experiences reported by the teachers in our professional development projects:

> "Students get very excited. Monday morning they come eager to see what is in the estimation jar for the week. They are good at guessing."

> "Students are using more math vocabulary. At mealtime I have heard them ask, 'How many ounces do you think this is?' with the milk we drink every day."

> "They are going around the room and experimenting. They are having conversations about [math], which is something I didn't see them do before."

> "When they start out, the children are not really that interested, but right now all you can see them doing is imitating us. I had four kids and every time another student came in the classroom, they would count how many children were there."

Seeing children demonstrate new understanding of a subject area or show an increase in their skills is another key motivator. That's why you teach: to make a difference for children and their families. It's exciting when you see growth in students who previously were struggling with the material. For example:

- "The children are counting by tens now. Our kids stand together and count to one hundred. Even their work in groups is great. Before, I didn't see that happening, but now I see a lot of growth in that."

- "I have seen kids be more confident in the answers they give, their counting, and everything."

- "A lot of our children whom we thought didn't know much have surprised us. . . . When you think the children are not listening, they turn around and surprise you."

Children's responses can inform or alter your expectations about what engages children and what children can actually do. If you've had doubts about new practices, you may begin to value those practices after seeing how children love them.

In addition to children's responses, feedback from other adults is valuable during the practice phase of growth. You and your fellow teachers learn from one another when you work together and when you have opportunities to connect in other classrooms, programs, or schools. You learn from being able to watch one another in action. Here are some thoughts from teachers about the power of learning from one another:

- "Having a good coteacher is helpful, watching and learning from her."

- "What changed my negative feelings about teaching early math was watching other teachers, how they do it and just trying out their strategies. Listening to the language they used, using the same language, and seeing how the kids reacted."

Mentors, coaches, and supervisors, too, can provide encouragement and new ideas, as these teachers found:

- "I get encouragement from my coach. If it wasn't for her, I don't think I would have gone broader in my teaching."

▶ "[The coach] pushed us to think out of our box, asking things like, 'Could you add this?' She encouraged us to experiment when we might not have taken that leap on our own."

You expand your horizons for learning when you have conversations with other teachers about carrying out new strategies. You recognize challenges you have in common. When you talk with teachers who have different teaching styles, you invite fresh ideas to your conversations. You learn from one another's problem-solving experiences. Knowing there is more than one way to approach a particular learning experience or challenge increases your options. Learning from one another provides everyone with ways to integrate the new information.

You and your fellow teachers learn from one another when you work together and when you have opportunities to connect in other classrooms, programs, or schools.

Hearing others' perspectives can help you reframe what you are seeing in your classroom, too. Sometimes, when you're in the midst of an interaction with a child, it is difficult to see the root of a challenge. Discussing that problem with others, or having others observe and share what they see, may help you see something you have missed, or see the situation from the child's or family's perspective.

Other teachers can also help you understand the impact of community context and culture on children's learning. Take the case of Awan, the teacher at the beginning of this chapter who was wondering how she might teach the concept of rhyme to some of the Hmong children in her group:

When Awan shared with other teachers at her site her observation that Hmong children were not understanding the concept of rhyme, she learned from a Hmong coworker that teaching rhyme to Hmong children might require a different approach. Awan decided to gather more information as she continued to try different strategies in her classroom. She met with a literacy specialist in her program who was Hmong. He suggested talking with the children's family members about rhyming. Awan invited him to the center's family literacy night to describe how rhyme was used in children's picture books in the classrooms. He created some nonsense rhymes in Hmong to use as playful examples for families and their children.

> **Guiding Questions:** **Getting and Using Feedback from Others**
>
> **As you try out new content and strategies, here are some questions to help you get and use feedback from others:**
>
> > What did the responses from others (children, families, or coworkers) tell you?
>
> > How could you improve your teamwork in this effort?
>
> > Do you have opportunities to share your challenges and problem-solve with colleagues?
>
> > How might context (program, community, culture, and so on) be affecting responses, or results, or your understanding of responses or results? How can you find out?
>
> > Has feedback offered you any ideas for adapting your approach?
>
> **If these questions raise concerns for you, think about ways to address your concerns:**
>
> > Continue to communicate with your team members about your strategies and goals.
>
> > Ask your colleagues what they see.
>
> > Ask team members if they would like to try a strategy or take the lead for a part of your lesson.

How Does This Phase of Growth Affect Your Daily Practice?

When you put new learning into practice, you make the learning your own. It becomes part of your teaching story. See the reproducible form "Short Story on Learning from Practice" on page 106 to explore how you have learned from practice.

Your Professional Identity: Who You Are as a Teacher

During the learning phase of growth, you may have felt you didn't have much control over what you were being asked to learn. In the practice phase of growth, you can take more control of your learning. This requires examining yourself honestly as a teacher and taking risks. You must try to see what's happening in your classroom from a variety of perspectives: that of the children in your classroom, that of the children's families, that of colleagues and coworkers, and that of coaches and supervisors.

The practice phase of growth calls for patience, persistence, and flexibility with yourself as well as with others. Teachers are often their own biggest critics. Although some people believe students succeed due to intelligence or inborn ability, recent research suggests that actually, students are more successful when they believe success is due to hard work, not innate qualities.[7] You will be more successful as a teacher if you approach your own learning in this manner. Remember that no one is born a good teacher. Just as you scaffold children's knowledge and skill, challenging them to the edge of their competence, so you should treat yourself as a learner. As you practice, you internalize and integrate new ways of thinking about learning and teaching. This process takes time and repetition.

Encountering Dilemmas: What and How You Practice

State your dilemmas explicitly so you can address them deliberately. Investing time and effort in conscious reflection helps you take ownership of your own learning. It also helps you resolve your dilemmas.

One dilemma of the practice phase of growth involves risk taking. As you practice new skills, you are taking risks in front of others or with others. When you change your instructional methods, you know your actions affect children, their families, or your coworkers. You may worry that a change in your educational approach will have a negative impact on others, especially children. Yet you know that children are also your primary motivator for trying new things and taking on challenges that enhance your teaching.

A second dilemma of the practice phase involves competing priorities. You may worry that the time and effort you spend practicing new strategies makes instructional time less productive in your classroom. This dilemma forces you to evaluate whether the change you're practicing is worth the potential disruptions or mistakes because it will bring greater rewards in the long run.

A third dilemma of the practice phase is that as teachers dig deeper into learning, the learning can become more difficult. Casey's story about searching for a way to help a child learn to count is a good example of how complex this phase can be. As Casey looked more closely at her goal, she realized she had to learn more about the development of counting skills as well as more techniques to support the skill. Your initial excitement about instructional change may fade as you realize how complicated learning is for children. As you experience success, you may also raise expectations for yourself and for others.

As you refine your new strategy through practice, you may experience as many failures as successes. You can use your mistakes or failures as opportunities to learn how to structure your activities more effectively.

Dealing with Feelings

During the practice phase of growth, you may struggle with your emotions. Even if you enjoy some aspects of wrestling with new or contradictory ideas, feeling off-balance is, by definition, uncomfortable. As you practice and learn more, sometimes you may feel competent—and at other times you may feel utterly at sea.

> Remember that no one is born a good teacher. Just as you scaffold children's knowledge and skill, challenging them to the edge of their competence, so you should treat yourself as a learner.

Reflecting on what works, what doesn't work, and why can be difficult when you judge yourself too harshly. If you tend to be self-critical, seek instead to reframe your perspective and think of yourself as a lifelong learner. Lifelong learners are curious, they wonder, and they step back and listen to other perspectives. They are never done learning, because learning is a continuous process. They work to learn from their mistakes.

As you try new strategies in the classroom, it is important to be persistent. Remind yourself to continue, even when you try a strategy and it doesn't go well. This is an opportunity to think more carefully about why your strategy didn't work the way you expected it would. Think about how you might adjust your approach, or simply try again. As one teacher put it, "Teaching is a huge experiment. I am always asking, 'Does this work?' and testing. It is a long learning process."

Sometimes teachers and program leaders forget that practicing new interactions takes time and persistence. Introduce new practices slowly rather than trying to change everything at once. Your patience will be rewarded. In the long run, these changes will benefit everyone in your classroom: the children, their families, other staff, and you. As one teacher explained:

> "It was a slow process: we slowly introduced numbers, and more visuals on the wall, and incorporated them. We had not previously had a math table—it combined science and math (so we added a math table). Then we added the estimation jar, which was fun. Once it got started, it got easier; things started to flow. Math was everywhere. Being more aware, (we) taught it more and in different ways, and it made the kids want to learn it more."

In Chapter 6, you will explore the third phase of your journey, Teachers Share and Model. Sharing and modeling provide opportunities for you to include others in your teaching story.

References

1. Jean Piaget, *Biology and Knowledge* (Chicago: University of Chicago Press, 1971): 176.

2. Judith Longfield, "Discrepant Teaching Events: Using an Inquiry Stance to Address Student's Misconceptions," *International Journal of Teaching and Learning in Higher Education* 21, no. 2 (2009): 266–271.

3. George Forman, "Mirrors That Talk: Using Video to Improve Early Education," *Connections* (January 2002): 1. eclkc.ohs.acf.hhs.gov/hslc/tta-system/teaching/eecd/domains%20of%20child%20development/science/mirrors.pdf.

4. Terry Borton, *Reach, Touch, and Teach: Student Concerns and Process Education* (New York: McGraw-Hill, 1970): 94–98.

5. Brian Mowry, "Engaging and Developing Young Children's Informal Number Sense" (presentation, Numbers Work! Institute, Saint Paul, MN, March 8, 2013).

6. Janet Jerve, "Janet's Story" (unpublished manuscript, September 19, 2014). Used with permission of the author.

7. Carol S. Dweck, *Mindset: The New Psychology of Success* (New York: Random House, 2006): 6–11.

Trying a New Strategy*

What?
What do you plan to try?

What do you think will happen?

↓

So What?
Did anything unexpected happen?

What worked? What didn't?

How do you know?

↓

Now What?
What do you want to change?

What do you want to repeat?

Do you need more information or resources?

* The "What? So What? Now What?" model is from Terry Borton. *Reach, Touch, and Teach: Student Concerns and Process Education* (New York: McGraw-Hill, 1970): 94–98. Used with permission of McGraw-Hill Education. From *Intentional Teaching in Early Childhood: Ignite Your Passion for Learning and Improve Outcomes for Young Children* by Sandra Heidemann, Beth Menninga, and Claire Chang, copyright © 2019. This page may be reproduced for individual, classroom, or small group work only. For other uses, contact Free Spirit Publishing Inc. at www.freespirit.com/permissions.

Short Story on Learning from Practice

Think about a memorable time when you tried something
in your classroom that didn't go well—at least the first time. What
did you do? What did others do? How did you feel? What did you do next?
Did you make any adjustments and try again, or did you try something
else? When you think about this experience now, what do you
learn from it (about the strategy, about children,
about teaching, or about yourself)? Write up
this story about your teaching practice.

6 TEACHERS SHARE AND MODEL

Abdi was nervous. She was about to present at her local Association for the Education of Young Children conference. She had submitted a proposal months earlier and was thrilled when the conference organizers accepted it. But now she was questioning her own expertise. A few weeks ago, she had shared with the teachers in her program several ways she integrated math into her daily routines. That had gone very well, but Abdi wasn't sure she could fill up ninety minutes with her ideas today, and she worried she would run out of things to say.

The third phase of the teacher's growth cycle is Teachers Share and Model, which builds on the first two phases, Teachers Learn and Teachers Practice. In the third phase of growth, you take what you have learned and practiced and share it with other teachers and with families. As you begin to present, train, or consult, you may want to change your career path and become a trainer, mentor, coach, or supervisor. But a career change is not necessary to influence others in the field. You can use your experience and knowledge to share and model in a variety of ways while still teaching young children in the classroom.

As a teacher, you can share with others in the following ways:

- sharing strategies in staff meetings
- leading discussions in team meetings
- modeling practices with other team members in their classrooms
- sharing what works and what doesn't work after an activity
- giving colleagues feedback on their teaching practices

- listening to colleagues talk about what they are trying with children
- modeling problem solving with team members when a strategy doesn't work
- inviting other teachers to observe you at work in your classroom
- sharing child development information with families
- suggesting activities families can do with their children
- modeling how to do activities for families
- presenting at conferences
- writing articles

You can see the list is a long one. Although presenting a workshop at a conference, as Abdi did, is one way to share what you have learned, it is by no means the only way to do so. Sharing what you have learned with others brings you many benefits. In this chapter you'll explore what you learn as you share and model. You'll also explore in more depth how it affects you.

What You Share and Model

Like many teachers, you probably know more than you realize. But if you work alone or with just one or two other adults, you may not often articulate what you know. You are likely very busy and thankful at the end of each day if things have gone mostly well. When you do begin to share what you know, you may realize that you have to make on-the-spot judgments many times a day. It is those judgments that other teachers are eager to hear about. For example, they want to know how you did an activity, what problems you encountered, and how you solved them. They want to know how you fit early math and literacy activities into your daily routines and how the children responded to these activities. They want to know how you carried out your program's social-emotional curriculum with the dual language learners in your class. Following are specific topics teachers often want to hear about from other teachers.

Teaching Strategies

Teaching strategies include everything from specific curricula to individual activities. Teachers want to know what engages children and if the strategies they're learning about are effective. A trainer's knowledge is helpful, and for teachers, it is critical to hear from other teachers how their read-alouds are going, how to use a number line, how they use graphing during their large and small groups, how they are approaching behavioral concerns, and so forth.

Routines

Teachers want to learn how they can use routines to teach conceptual material in a fun and engaging way. Beginning teachers may feel that daily routines are tasks to simply get through. Routines may seem like wasted time. But when teachers hear how some classrooms use routines to strengthen learning, they get inspired to think up their own such ideas. For example, dressing for outdoor weather in cold climates can be time-consuming and frustrating for adults and children alike. In one classroom, teachers introduced a sequencing activity to help children get dressed. They instructed children:

1. Put on your snow pants.

2. Put on your coat.

3. Put on your boots.

4. Put on your hat.

5. Put on your mittens.

The teachers reinforced this sequence every day. As the children learned the sequence, dressing for outside play became easier. Meanwhile, the children were learning a valuable skill for both literacy and math: putting events in order. Counting during transitions and rhyming when groups leave the classroom are additional ways to reinforce children's learning during daily routines.

Environments

Arranging a classroom requires decisions, decisions, decisions. Some of the questions that teachers may have are:

 ⬤ Do I put the blocks and dramatic play close together?

 ⬤ How many materials should I put in the math center?

▶ Should I limit the number of children in each area?

▶ Should the library be near the writing center?

▶ What do I do with that strangely shaped nook?

With so many decisions to make about how to arrange the classroom and what to put in the learning centers, teachers may forget about representing early math and literacy throughout the classroom. Or they may put so many manipulatives or games in the math center that children are overwhelmed. Or they may forget to refresh their classrooms as the year progresses. When teachers share both their questions and their solutions, children benefit.

The Thinking Behind Instructional Decisions

Because of their busy schedules both at work and at home, teachers rarely get a chance to share how they think about what they are teaching. When teachers can set aside time to really talk about developmentally appropriate practice, about how integrating math and literacy into instruction benefits students and reduces the achievement gap, about how new strategies work with their program's social-emotional curriculum, and about other philosophical issues, teachers understand at a deeper level what they are doing with young children in the classroom. Such reflection gives teachers more flexibility to address children's learning. Teachers are better able to reflect in this way if they hear the concerns, questions, and dilemmas of other teachers.

Engaging Families

Teachers want to hear how other teachers have engaged families in their children's learning. Sharing ideas, strategies, and problems helps teachers be more effective. They can help one another examine their assumptions about parents and other family members. Sometimes teachers assume families don't really care when they haven't been as responsive as teachers would like. But the reality might be very different. Family members can feel intimidated, be busy with several jobs, or be unsure of how to approach activities sent home from school. For instance, teachers in one center were concerned about low family involvement in their children's math learning. The teachers found that their students' parents got excited about math when they were given specific ideas for how to do the activities and saw their children's enthusiasm for the activities.

Teachers also want to know how other teachers share their expertise with families. When teachers compare notes, they find that some teachers send home notes suggesting activities families can do to help children learn the concepts they are teaching in school. They also can send home newsletters with descriptions of class projects and field trips. Teachers can model how to play games and demonstrate read-alouds during family nights. Some teachers post signs in the classroom telling about what children are learning in the different centers. This approach helps family members understand what is going on when they visit the classroom.

Finally, teachers want to know how other teachers communicate with families. Through discussion with colleagues, teachers learn how listening to what family members say about their children's interests and experiences provides valuable information to help both children and their families.

This sharing and modeling phase of growth requires a different set of skills than learning and practicing do. It also requires a willingness to grapple with different questions and possibilities. See the reproducible form "Sharing and Modeling: From Comfort to Confidence" on pages 127–128. This form can help you reflect on your own comfort level with sharing and modeling.

Developing Confidence

In this third phase of growth, you have more confidence in your grasp of the content and the effectiveness of the strategies you are learning and practicing. You own your learning and are eager to experiment with the activities you have tried.

In a way, this third phase is an extension of the second phase, Teachers Practice. You are still trying new ways of reaching students, engaging families, and learning new strategies. However, now you are willing to share with other teachers what you know and do. You feel confident enough to let others see how your classroom is organized, how your strategies are structured, and how you have adapted activities based on children's responses. You know how to solve problems. When an activity doesn't go well, you no longer see yourself as a failure; you look for ways to improve it. You have learned how to read assessment data and plan from it. You know that if you decide on a goal based on how children are actually doing, you can find strategies that work. In other words, you are confident you can help children learn conceptual material, which will help them succeed as they move into the next challenge, whether that is to a new skill, a new grade, or a new school.

After participating in a math initiative, one teacher reflected, "I think I got more confidence, and felt more eager to get the children involved in learning math. Before participating, I didn't think of what I could do to teach the children math besides counting numbers. In the present, we have music and more games that are age-appropriate."

Even as you feel more confident in your teaching abilities, this third phase of growth can throw you into a new crisis of confidence. You may wonder if your experience and your strategies will be helpful and valuable to other teachers. The thought of sharing with other adults may bring up new doubts about your skills. You may question your ability to present or write. You may fear presenting to a large group.

> Regardless of whether you tend to be an extrovert or introvert, you have valuable experience and information to share.

How you approach this phase of your growth may depend partly on your personality type. People all fall somewhere on an extrovert-introvert spectrum, and where you fall can also depend on the situation and how comfortable you feel in it. Extroverts seek out new experiences, are often the first people to speak up in a group, and enjoy meeting new people. Introverts may watch and wait before jumping into interactions with others, seek out people they already know in a group, and think carefully before responding to requests or questions.[1]

If you tend to be an extrovert, you may find this phase of growth exciting. You may feel eager to present, participate in discussions, and share your strategies. If you tend to be an introvert, you may shy away from presenting to a group of teachers. You may feel uncomfortable speaking up in a staff meeting to share your thoughts, struggles, and strategies. Regardless of whether you tend to be an extrovert or introvert, you have valuable experience and information to share. Either way, embrace the new opportunities before you in this phase.

> **Guiding Questions:** **Developing Confidence**
>
> **As you develop confidence in your ability to share and model what you know, here are some questions to ponder:**
>
> > What do you gain when you watch other teachers present their teaching practices in either formal or informal settings?
>
> > What hopes or fears would arise if you were asked to demonstrate a teaching strategy to other teachers?
>
> > What might you learn about your teaching from presenting to other teachers?
>
> > Describe supports that would help you prepare to demonstrate or present a teaching strategy to other teachers.
>
> **If these questions raise concerns for you, think about ways to address them:**
>
> > If you are hesitant to share with other teachers, find ways to start small. Meet with teachers in your program and share with them in an informal setting. Do a small five-minute presentation at a staff meeting. Present with others; sharing the responsibility and the stage with colleagues can make speaking in front of others less intimidating.
>
> > Think about what is helpful for you to hear from other teachers and plan a presentation on that subject.
>
> > Remember, sharing your practices can include showing as well as telling. You may prefer to invite a colleague who is interested in one of your teaching strategies to come and teach with you for a day.

Sharing Content and Strategies

In the third phase of growth, you already have a foundation of knowledge and skill in the content area you are learning. As you share and model your knowledge and skills, you deepen your learning through questioning, reflection, and reexamination.

Presenting and writing can help you go deeper in your learning. That's because when you have to explain a strategy to others, you must examine your own understanding of it. When you have to put the idea into words, you must think through the steps you took to plan and introduce the strategy. You have to reply to questions from others about how children responded. You must articulate what changes or adaptations you made from trial and error.

Planning presentations or writing up ideas requires you to look at the information and skills you have mastered in a new way. You have to think through each step, keeping in mind what others will want or need to know in order to understand your ideas. As you work to spell out each step you have taken, previously understood concepts may become murky. You may question your current interpretation, and in the process, reorganize your thinking about the information as you arrive at a deeper understanding.

The experience we had with one early math concept, cardinality, demonstrates how this reorganization works. (Cardinality is the idea that the last number counted in a set of items represents the amount of items in the set.) Teachers readily understood cardinality when we described it in a workshop. But neither we nor our audience of teachers knew what cardinality really meant for young children. Cardinality as an understanding of the number of objects in a group was not part of any of our child development frameworks. We kept circling back to this concept in trainings and goal-setting sessions. It took months of repeated explorations before we understood what cardinality looked like when children had mastered the concept and what it looked like when they hadn't. Gradually, cardinality became part of the teachers'—and our—early math frameworks. As teachers shared observations of what cardinality looked like in their students, they could assess its development more easily.

Sometimes, new information may conflict with your previous thinking about an idea. For instance, if you are working on a presentation about shapes and spatial sense, you may find that approaches to teaching the names of the shapes have changed since you were a child in school. When new information does not align with old information, you experience *cognitive dissonance*—the mental discomfort of holding two or more contradictory ideas at the same time. Something like this happened in a training session we conducted on shapes and spatial awareness, when we shared the following definitions of rectangles and squares:

▶ Rectangles are shapes with four straight sides, in which all four angles are right angles and opposite sides have the same length.

❭ Squares are one kind of rectangle in which all four sides have the same length.

Some teachers refused to accept that squares were a special kind of rectangle, because they had been taught that rectangles and squares were two distinct shapes. In their mental frameworks, squares and rectangles were different shapes and had to be taught that way. These teachers were confused, puzzled, and resistant to the new idea that squares are rectangles. They didn't want to confuse the children. They couldn't figure out how to explain that a square is a rectangle. After much discussion, they started to see the logic of the newer approach. We talked about different ways they could introduce the shapes with the new language. As they integrated this new information, their understanding of shapes transformed.

As you share with other adults, you aren't the only one integrating new information internally. You also encourage other teachers to integrate new thinking and try new strategies. All this rethinking contributes to teachers' cognitive growth.

Guiding Questions: Sharing Content and Strategies

Here are some guiding questions to ponder as you share content and strategies with others:

❭ What type of information do you want to share with others (for example, a teaching strategy, an assessment strategy, an insight into curriculum)?

❭ Does the information you will share require rethinking current assumptions? If so, how might you help others wrestle with this new idea?

❭ If you are sharing a teaching strategy or process, what are the steps you would share with others? For example:
- What do you need to plan and prepare before you start?
- How do you introduce the strategy to children?
- What have you observed about children's responses?
- What are some adjustments you made to the strategy and why?
- Are there any next steps?

> **If these questions raise concerns for you, think about ways to address them:**
>
> ❯ When you are going to present to other teachers, prepare what you are going to say and the materials you will need. Practice in front of the mirror to help you feel less nervous.
>
> ❯ Keep it simple by starting with just one or two ideas, and include details in your presentation. Teachers like to know how you introduce an activity and what likely responses they may see from the children.
>
> ❯ Sharing details about how and why your own thinking has changed may help others process new information.
>
> ❯ If you don't want to present, you can share and model your expertise in other ways. Plan to share informally with other teachers at staff meetings, at team meetings, or individually. Share ideas on social media sites where teachers exchange concrete teaching strategies.

Engaging Other Adults

In this phase of growth, you are learning how to engage other adults. Presenting, writing, and other forms of sharing are about content, but they are also about engaging an audience of adult learners. Adults bring life experience to their learning and teaching. When you are learning to work with adults, you need to learn how to acknowledge and use that experience to further challenge them.

Someone moving from teaching children to teaching adults must use new instructional techniques. While the goal of engaging the learners is the same, the *way* you engage the different learners requires different sets of skills. Some techniques for teaching adults are:

- providing hands-on activities
- providing opportunities for discussion
- acknowledging and valuing previous experience
- connecting theory to practice

- providing demonstrations through video or in person
- providing strategies that teachers can easily carry out in the classroom
- breaking down strategies into smaller steps to illustrate how to plan and implement

You need the encouragement and support of others to successfully navigate this phase of growth. Even if you feel very confident in your abilities with children in the classroom, you may be afraid of failing when you're working with other adults. Supervisors, directors, colleagues, and friends can all be supporters. They can push, prod, and cheer you on as you consider how you want to share your skills. For example, one teacher noted, "Our literacy coach really opened the door for me to see myself differently. I would never have thought I could do this or that. I have blossomed more than I ever expected."

> Adults bring life experience to their learning and teaching. When you are learning to work with adults, you need to learn how to acknowledge and use that experience to further challenge them.

During this phase of growth, you also develop your ability to engage and involve families in the children's learning. You learn what activities will be successful at home. You do the activities at school first, so the children understand what is expected and can teach their parents and other family members. You use family nights to demonstrate and model the activities in a nonthreatening way.

Even if you aren't presenting or writing up your experiences, you can model for other teachers in your team and your program. Your modeling gives other teachers ideas for their own work. As you model, children may not respond as you expected. Sharing this experience helps you and your colleagues accept the variability of groups. You begin to understand how to adapt strategies for differences in group composition, such as groups including dual language learners or children with special needs. Such openness forms the foundation of a learning community. As one teacher pointed out, "Each teacher brings something different to the table, and when you are in the classroom, you learn from each other's strengths and weaknesses."

Guiding Questions: **Engaging Other Adults**

Here are some guiding questions to ponder as you engage other adults by sharing and modeling with them:

> What are some ways you already share teaching ideas with other teachers?

> What do you value about ideas and strategies shared by other teachers?

> What are some ways in which exploring a strategy with adults is different from doing so with children?

> In what ways would exploring a strategy with adults be similar to doing so with children?

> If your audience is made up of coworkers or other people you know, what type of presentation works best for them?

> Might others (a coteacher, mentor, coach, or colleague from another program) be willing to present with you?

If these questions raise concerns for you, think about ways to address them:

> Ask fellow teachers and team members to present with you; this can help reduce the pressure and work.

> Think of what you find helpful in workshops and presentations and try to incorporate those elements into yours.

> Use a variety of formats when you're presenting, including demonstrations, make-it-and-take-it activities, and discussions.

> If you use social media, consider exploring and sharing teaching ideas online.

How Does This Phase of Growth Affect Your Daily Practice?

You may enter this phase of growth without even realizing it. It will probably happen when others ask you to share what you know. You may do so through formal presentations or through informal sharing and modeling in the classroom. In either case, those around you are acknowledging your skill. This may be a new experience for you if you have been concentrating on the children in your classroom, rather than interacting with a broader early childhood community. Although this opportunity to share what you've learned may be uncomfortable at first, it will challenge you in ways that will make you a better teacher.

When you are first sharing your skills, you may feel your presentations or demonstrations pull you away from the classroom. Whether you are mentoring other teachers, preparing presentations, or writing about your experiences, it takes time to plan what you will say and how you will say it. You will need to decide what materials to include in workshops and what examples to use. You may need to practice before you present or make games and worksheets to share with participants.

Even though your preparation will be time-consuming, you will find it very valuable to your work in the classroom. It offers you an opportunity to further integrate what you've learned about content and how content connects to strategies. You will find yourself thinking about how you structured your activities to ensure success and may come up with even more creative ways to engage students. As you define terms, you may find that you have questions about a specific definition or that you can't provide a good example from your classroom. These challenges push you to think more deeply about what you know and how you teach.

When you are in this phase, you may interact with teachers from other settings. They may have different philosophies or practices. They may refer to unfamiliar standards or administrative structures. You may compare yourself to them in terms of education and experience. You will gain more confidence as you realize how much you have to offer.

Your Professional Identity: Who You Are as a Teacher

This phase of growth consolidates your professional identity. As an early childhood educator, you have a solid grasp of child development, curriculum, academic content, teaching strategies, and assessment. You know how to develop a warm, trusting relationship with children and how to adapt instruction to their individual needs. Now you are sharing your knowledge of teaching and learning with others. In doing this, you receive recognition and respect for what you know.

When you share with others, you become a teacher leader. School leaders such as principals, superintendents, and coaches are often seen as instructional leaders, but teachers are leaders as well. As a teacher leader, you provide an example to inspire other teachers. You share your successes and failures and demonstrate your commitment to teaching and learning every day. You can answer concrete questions about activities and how children responded. Following are a few of the roles you perform as a teacher leader:*

> **Resource provider.** You lend materials and toys to other teachers. You share websites, books, articles, and lesson plans.

> **Instructional specialist.** When you share strategies and activities for content areas, such as literacy and math, or when you share techniques that have helped children function better in the learning environment, you are an instructional specialist.

> **Classroom supporter.** You support other teachers when you work alongside them in the classroom, model strategies for them, and observe and give feedback to them.

> **Data coach.** If you understand and use data effectively for planning, you can help other teachers understand and use their data as well.

> **Catalyst for change.** You continue to ask questions and push for excellence.

Your commitment to teaching and lifelong learning will be evident to all, including you, as you listen to teachers' stories, share your strategies and resources, and help teachers understand and plan from their data. To think more deeply about your leadership skills, complete the reproducible form "How Are You a Teacher Leader?" on page 129.

As a teacher leader, you provide an example to inspire other teachers.

---

* Reprinted with permission of Education Leadership Copyright Clearance. All rights reserved. Cindy Harrison and Joellen Killion, "Ten Roles for Teacher Leaders," *Educational Leadership*, 65, no. 1 (2007): 74–77.

Encountering Dilemmas: What and How You Practice

As in all the other phases of growth, you will encounter dilemmas as you develop training or share strategies. Learning to train other teachers involves as many decisions as teaching children in the classroom. These decisions will bring up dilemmas.

What Content to Include

When you are planning your training or your meeting with another teacher, you need to decide how much you want to share. It's helpful to make your teaching personal by sharing a little about yourself, but it is more important to hear what questions your audience has. In other words: you can tell stories, but keep them short and to the point.

You will need to ask yourself if hearing about your struggles would further teachers' growth. Do you want to lay bare some of your earlier dilemmas, such as academic versus social-emotional content? Do you want to share the disagreement you had with your team members about the implementation of strategies? Will it violate confidentiality if you speak about your team members?

What Kinds of Materials

You will want to use a variety of methods so teachers can access the material regardless of their preferred learning styles. Some people learn best by seeing, some by listening, and some by touching and doing. Make sure you have visual, auditory, and kinesthetic activities at the ready. You may feel overwhelmed by the amount of information you want to share and be tempted to lecture, but if you present the information in a variety of ways, participants are more likely to retain it. Other decisions you will need to make beforehand or on the spot are:

- Should I open up my presentation for questions?
- How much discussion should I include?
- How much lecturing should I do?
- What kinds of visual aids should I use?
- What kinds of materials do I want to demonstrate?

Handling Comments and Challenges

When you present your ideas and experiences to others, you open yourself up to comments, suggestions, and criticism. Other teachers may challenge your ideas. Think about how you will handle this feedback. Watch other presenters to see how they handle the feedback. Although these types of dialogues can be difficult, they will help you and other teachers verbalize and wrestle with cognitive conflicts.

Balancing Commitments

If you find yourself presenting often, you may ask yourself if you are spending too much time out of your classroom. Sharing and modeling while teaching is a balancing act. You will need to check often to see if the balance is working for you.

Following is a story told by a teacher, Gwen. Gwen was excited about teaching children and learning new strategies in the classroom. But she didn't expect to be presenting her ideas to other teachers in a workshop. She shares what she learned about herself in the process of sharing and modeling.*

> I am a shy person and I usually don't like to have all the attention on me, but I was excited to be asked to present a math activity at math training in March for about sixty early childhood teachers. The activity I chose to teach involved using an estimation jar and a number line to help preschool children understand more about numbers.
>
> When children in my classroom arrive in the morning, they each guess how many items are in the estimation jar. A teacher helps the children write their guesses next to their names on the whiteboard in the group area. On the whiteboard there is also a large one-through-twenty number line that everyone can see. During large-group time, I ask the children to help me figure out how many items there are in the jar by counting and using the number line.
>
> When I was preparing for the training, I thought, "The children are the stars. The best way to teach others is to show them what we do." I was allowed only ten minutes to present my training, so we decided to record a five-minute video to save time for discussion and questions. I wasn't nervous being recorded, because I wasn't interested in showing something that was perfect. I wanted it to be

---

* Gwen Dobson, 2014. Used with permission of the author.

real. The number line and estimation jar activity is a process I had developed with the children since the beginning of the year. Over time I had learned what children liked, what motivated them, and what they needed from me to help them understand. The children and I had become a community of learners. We had ownership of our process. I had had so much practice, I knew how to handle all levels of learners, how to encourage older children to help teach younger ones, and how to make sure every child's effort felt like a success. If I had been asked to present this in September, I would have said no, but at this point in the year I was ready.

I presented four times as teachers rotated through my session. Each time, they asked good questions and seemed very interested. I could see how excited they were, and some of them came up to me later to tell me they were going to try my approach with their class. It made me feel really good. I thought, "Even little old me can bring something important and exciting to share with other teachers."

Gwen's Estimation Jar Routine

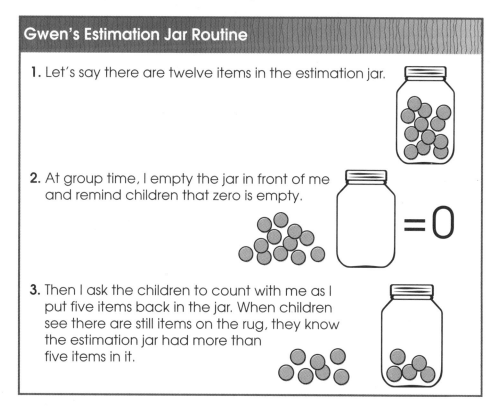

1. Let's say there are twelve items in the estimation jar.

2. At group time, I empty the jar in front of me and remind children that zero is empty.

3. Then I ask the children to count with me as I put five items back in the jar. When children see there are still items on the rug, they know the estimation jar had more than five items in it.

4. Then I ask the children to look at the number written next to each child's name on the whiteboard to find what numbers we can erase.

Justin 6
Dante 10
Jamar 12
Adadi 2
Homer 9
Maryann 9
Sai 3
Joseph 2
Allen 13

5. A child helper erases all guesses from one through five.

Justin 6
Dante 10
Jamar 12
Adadi
Homer 9
Maryann 9
Sai
Joseph
Allen 13

6. Next we count five more items into the jar, counting up from five to ten. The class now knows there were more than ten items in the jar, and again the helper erases the guesses from five through ten.

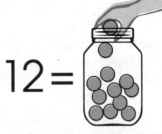

Justin
Dante 10
Jamar 12
Adadi
Homer
Maryann
Sai
Joseph
Allen 13

7. Finally we count in the two remaining items, and the children now know there were twelve items in the jar.

$$12 =$$

8. The class looks to see who guessed twelve. This person or the closest guesser usually gets a sticker.

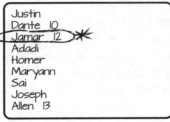

Justin
Dante 10
Jamar 12
Adadi
Homer
Maryann
Sai
Joseph
Allen 13

9. The child helper or teacher marks the number twelve to show everyone where twelve is on the number line. Again, we look at the whiteboard for guesses that were more than twelve. I select one and mark it on the number line. We talk about twelve and guesses that were more than twelve and less than twelve and how to find them on the number line.

```
Justin
Dante  10
Jamar  12  *
Adadi
Homer
Maryann
Sai
Joseph
Allen  13
```

```
1  2  3  4  5  6  7  8  9  10 11  12 13
```

Dealing with Feelings

When you begin to share your experiences and expertise with teachers, you may feel inadequate. You are probably very aware of how your strategies succeed in engaging children some days, but also keenly aware that there are other days when it seems that nothing goes right. Don't be afraid to share these realities. This type of acknowledgment builds trust with other teachers. They are more likely to try your activities if they believe in your authenticity. It is helpful to remember you are not an expert. If someone asks you a question you cannot answer, say you will look it up (and then do look it up and get back to the person about it). Show others that you are always learning. When you do, you give them the freedom to be learners as well.

As you share and model, you are taking risks. You are pushing through doubts about your competence. You may feel uncomfortable speaking in front of a group or presenting during a meeting. These are all normal feelings that happen as you take steps toward growth.

Your feelings and how you respond to them may vary depending on whether you are an extrovert or an introvert. An extrovert may jump in and volunteer quickly to present at a staff meeting, while an introvert may sit back and wait to see how it goes for others first. Extroverts and introverts can learn from one another. If you are an extrovert, wait before you jump into a discussion or volunteer to present. See if other teachers are ready but feeling hesitant, and just need encouragement to share their activities. If you are an introvert, volunteer to present and see what happens. Choose an activity you have done many times with results you are confident about.

Steps for a Successful Presentation

1. Decide on the information you want to share. It is better to start with a narrower focus than a broader one.

2. Make an outline of your presentation.

3. Plan to have about ten minutes of lecture at a time, then a hands-on activity or discussion.

4. Design activities that reach all learners. For visual learners, have handouts and PowerPoint presentations. For auditory learners, read parts of the handouts out loud; offer tapes or other learning aids if possible. For kinesthetic learners, include activities that get the group moving, such as games, music and movement, and walkabouts (in which participants move around the room to different tables to add to brainstorming lists).

5. Use humor and stories about children to help participants relax and relate to your material.

6. Practice your presentation so you feel freer to adapt it if necessary.

7. Distribute an evaluation to help you learn what you want to keep and what you want to change.

8. Enjoy yourself!

Now that you have learned about the three phases you go through as you grow and become more mindful in your instruction, you can use this knowledge to help you as you encounter new challenges. But remember that growth is not a journey you take alone. To successfully navigate the bumps and curves of learning, you will need support. In the next chapter, we explore the kinds of supports that will help you succeed.

References

1. Susan Cain, *Quiet: The Power of Introverts in a World That Can't Stop Talking* (New York: Crown Publishing Group, 2013): 11.

Sharing and Modeling:
From Comfort to Confidence

I am most comfortable sharing **one-on-one** when:		I would be more confident sharing **one-on-one** if:
I am most comfortable sharing in a **small group** when:		I would be more confident sharing in a **small group** if:
I am most comfortable sharing in a **larger group** when:		I would be more confident sharing in a **larger group** if:
I am most comfortable sharing by **copresenting** when:		I would be more confident sharing by **copresenting** if:

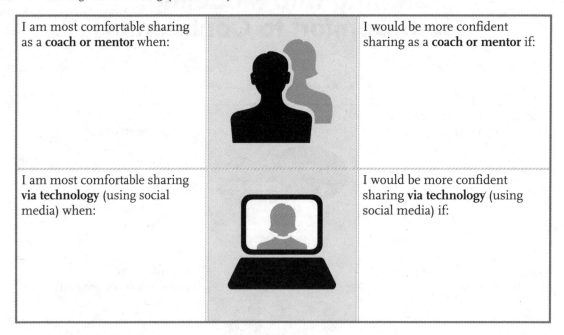

I am most comfortable sharing as a **coach or mentor** when:		I would be more confident sharing as a **coach or mentor** if:
I am most comfortable sharing **via technology** (using social media) when:		I would be more confident sharing **via technology** (using social media) if:

Questions for Reflection

1. **What patterns do you see in situations where you feel comfortable?**

2. **What patterns do you see in situations where you feel confident?**

3. **What do these patterns tell you about the supports you need to develop your skills and strategies?**

How Are You a Teacher Leader?

Teachers can take on several roles as teacher leaders:

- resource provider
- instructional specialist
- classroom supporter
- data coach
- catalyst for change

Look over these roles and answer the following questions as you think about the kinds of roles you play at work. You may not even realize how influential you are as a leader.

Which roles have you played in the past?

What did you enjoy about these roles?

What was difficult?

What would you like to do next?

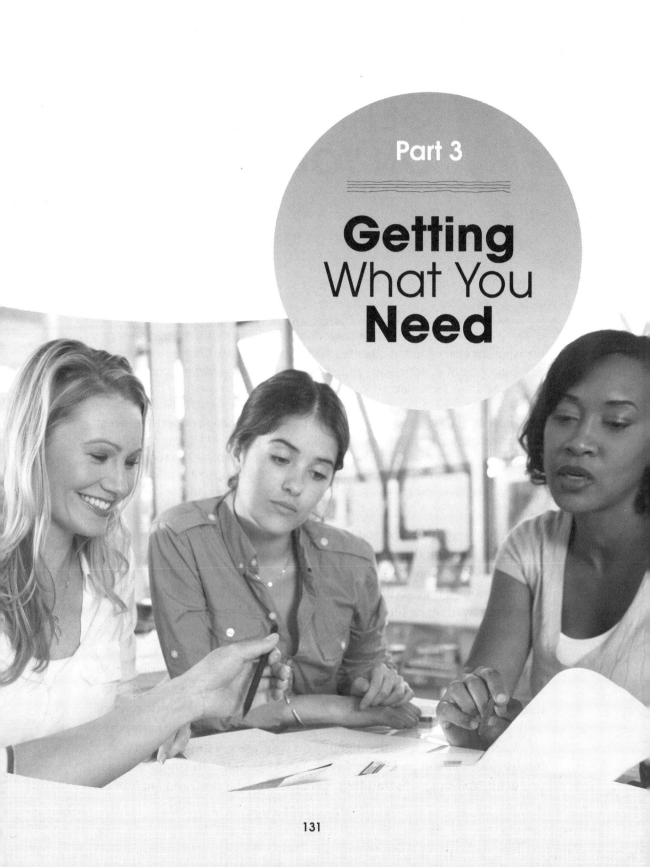

Part 3

Getting
What You
Need

7 GETTING SUPPORTS
ON YOUR JOURNEY

Chantelle had just finished participating in a three-year early literacy training project. Her director had sent her to the trainings so that she could present what she learned to the other teachers in her program. Chantelle was excited about what she had learned and was eager to share it with her colleagues. She planned two presentations, one on writing centers and another on phonological awareness. Everyone listened politely, but afterward Chantelle saw no evidence of changes in their everyday practice. She sat down with her director and expressed her frustration. Her director listened and then wondered aloud whether the other teachers needed more support to make the suggested changes. Together Chantelle and her director came up with a new plan to introduce early literacy to the staff and reinforce it during the whole year.

Throughout this book, you have explored your personal journey as a teacher. Although this journey is personal, it's not a journey you take alone, without support. For example, in the story above, Chantelle and her director realized they couldn't just tell the other teachers about Chantelle's experiences with early literacy and then expect them to carry out the strategies in their classroom. The teachers needed more training, some coaching, a chance to try the strategies, and opportunities to assess the children's progress. As Chantelle reflected on her own journey, she remembered that she herself needed time, resources, and practice before she was ready to introduce new early literacy strategies to her coworkers. If her coworkers were going to adopt these strategies, they would need the same supports.

Although you can work diligently on your own to improve your instruction, you will go further faster if you have built-in supports where you work. You can go to trainings, get advanced degrees, and analyze the results of your work with children, but feedback from colleagues, coaches, or supervisors about the curriculum, activities, and children's responses to the activities is invaluable when you are making instructional changes. With this feedback, you can practice and refine your strategies more effectively. It is difficult to transfer what you have learned without some ongoing support following training.[1] The journey from theory to practice, or the change from thinking differently to acting differently in your classroom, is more effective and comprehensive when you have support.

Perhaps you have never thought about the kinds of supports you need to deepen your knowledge and refine your practice. Like many teachers, you may operate largely on your own. By discovering how you learn best and what you need to maintain and deepen your learning, you can work with your supervisor and your employer to assemble the reinforcements you need. You'll need supports that connect you to ongoing learning and exploration—such as training, an understanding of your learning preferences, a learning community or community of practice, coaching, resources, building partnerships with families, and organizational supports.

Training

When you are first learning a new subject area, training is the typical starting place. Teacher training is often a onetime event. You might attend a daylong workshop and listen to a presenter lecture about a topic. Or your director may send you to a two-hour workshop and then expect you to present new ideas or content to the rest of the staff. While presenters or trainers may demonstrate strategies or have discussion groups, beyond that, few active learning experiences are likely to be offered. You may be expected to carry out what you've learned over the following week. However, our experience as trainers tells us this sort of quick, onetime training is the least effective way for teachers to learn new content and strategies. Research confirms our observations. Professional development is more likely to be effective when it:

- is given more than one time
- involves active learning
- is specific and detailed about concepts
- is given in a group already working together[2]

Through our professional development projects, we have learned that training planned with these four points in mind is more effective and brings about more change in teacher practices.

Training Given More Than One Time

We have discovered that teachers learn best when they're exposed to new content over time. For example, in the beginning of our math project (see Introduction, page 1), we did longer introductory trainings on early math content, but then we did shorter continuing workshops over three years that explored the math focal points in more depth. This repeated, consistent, and prolonged exposure helped teachers consolidate their observations of children and how children were learning math. They heard about the same math concepts at all trainings, but understood the concepts differently as time went by and they tried the math activities with children. Teachers could question the material, because they had experience to back them up.

Training with Active Learning

All our trainings involved active learning. We included strategies that we either demonstrated or invited teachers to practice during the training. We included many brainstorming sessions and discussion topics in the trainings. During data debriefings, we asked teachers to reflect on the strategies they used during the year and how their strategies affected the results and the children. One teacher confessed, "I was leery; I thought, 'How are you going to get preschoolers that involved?' But after the guest speakers at the trainings, after watching them and looking at the videos, I thought, 'I can do that.'"

Training That's Specific and Detailed About Concepts

We included specific details about the concepts we were covering. For example, in our early math project, we covered the early math focal points in a general way at first, but in all subsequent trainings we included very specific math information and definitions. We defined the math concepts and connected them to strategies in the classroom. During observations, we reinforced how we saw teachers carrying out the strategies and how these strategies were connected to the definitions. Because we made the information very specific to the classroom and to young children, teachers could see clearly how to structure lessons in a variety of learning formats. Trainers often provided materials during the trainings, so teachers could try the strategies immediately. As one teacher commented, "The trainings gave me knowledge I could bring back to my classroom."

Training Given in a Group Already Working Together

We took much of our ongoing training to the centers or schools where the teachers taught. We trained the entire staff together as much as possible. Because we gave the information to all teaching staff, including aides and assistants, children received similar feedback and scaffolding from a variety of people. All staff members can become more effective with children if they are given the opportunity to receive training, coaching, and support.[3]

Coworkers can help one another learn new strategies, help one another evaluate how a lesson is going, and support one another through the good and the bad. They can help clarify the definitions and create an atmosphere of excitement about learning. A teacher in one of our projects later explained, "We had assistants attend, so we were all on the same page. They had more confidence and could help plan."

The teachers in our project also had opportunities to attend conferences and institutes where they learned about current research and discovered new ideas about instruction, a variety of content areas, and classroom activities. The teachers spoke with other teachers about what they had tried and how it had or hadn't worked. The exhibit halls were often filled with new equipment and activities. Even when the teachers couldn't afford to buy the new equipment, seeing it gave them ideas for activities they could make.

The way we planned and implemented our training contributed to teachers' growth. You, too, can put these ideas into practice. If you are working on learning new techniques on your own or working with your program to plan professional development, think about the following as you go forward:

▶ If you want to learn about a new content area such as early literacy, early math, or a new curriculum, plan to go to trainings over time. Go to an introductory session, but then supplement that with trainings throughout the year. Repetition helps you process the information, and more importantly, it helps you apply what you have learned to strategies that work with children.

▶ Think about ways you can influence those who plan your staff training. Share lists of trainings with colleagues and supervisors—especially trainings that deal with a topic the staff is interested in, such as social-emotional development or challenging behaviors. Talk with them about how you and others on staff learn best. Tell them when you feel you need more training on a topic.

▶ After you attend a training with your coworkers, share what you learned (challenges and successes) as you apply new strategies into your daily teaching practice. Sometimes teachers are afraid to admit they aren't understanding a strategy or technique, but by doing so you open up space for your colleagues to also share their struggles. By sharing your struggles with a particular training, you can learn together and deepen your learning.

▶ Look for trainings that include active learning strategies, such as make-it-and-take-it, discussions, and movement. Make sure your instructor describes activities for children, too.

▶ Ask questions if your instructor is vague about what or how children are learning.

▶ If you can't participate in professional development with your coworkers, consider forming a learning community or community of practice on your own with other teachers (see page 141).

▶ If you attend or plan to attend a training outside of work, let colleagues and supervisors know what you find valuable about the content, mode of presentation, or the presenter. Volunteer to help plan or lead ongoing conversations about training content, such as through a book group.

See the reproducible form titled "Training Preferences" on pages 153–154. This worksheet will aid you in understanding what types of training help you succeed as a learner.

Learning Preferences

As you consider trainings in different content areas, think also about how you best learn and remember information. If you are aware of your learning preferences, you can take advantage of useful learning opportunities.

Elements of Effective Training

The following factors help you remember new content and carry out changes:

- how much the content builds on what you already know and do
- how much the underlying theory is linked to practice
- how many different concepts you are learning and how related they are to one another
- how many opportunities you have to practice, and then process, what you learn
- how many opportunities you have for feedback and problem solving as you apply the new knowledge (learning community or community of practice, coaching or mentoring, or reflective supervision)
- how deeply you explore the content by asking questions as you apply the content to your practice

Three Processes of Learning

There are many frameworks for thinking about how you learn. One useful model identifies three processes of learning used by both adults and children in early childhood education: direct instruction (verbal or reading), observation (modeling), and self-constructed learning (action and reflection).[4] You can probably identify knowledge and skills you have gained through each of these processes. For example, you may have listened to a conference keynote on brain development (direct instruction) and walked away with a better understanding of why some children react to stress in particular ways. It is likely that you have adopted some of your teaching strategies from watching other teachers in action (observation and modeling). You construct your own knowledge every day when you reflect on your day and use those reflections to inform your lesson plan for the next day (action and reflection). Although you use all these modes of learning, you probably prefer one over the others. Perhaps you prefer to learn about children's development through observation in the classroom. However, it is helpful to supplement your observations with readings that challenge or support your views.

Individual Learning Styles

Another framework to explore how you learn is individual learning styles. Individual learning styles help us understand the way we best hear, process, and retain information. Many people have one preferred learning style. Trainings that are structured to accommodate the style you prefer tend to stick with you longer. The three basic learning styles are as follows (though some models are more elaborate):

▶ visual

▶ auditory

▶ kinesthetic or tactile

Visual learners remember information best when they can see it. If they only hear it, they don't remember it as well. Auditory learners need to *hear* information, not just see it. They pay attention to voice tone, inflections, and the speed at which words are spoken. This helps them process the language. Kinesthetic or tactile learners learn best when they are moving, doing, and touching things. They like to make things and practice strategies during workshops. They get frustrated with too much talking.[5]

If you are aware of your learning style as a participant, you can let trainers or supervisors know your preferences. You can ask for more handouts, charts, or videos if you are a visual learner. If you are an auditory learner, you might reinforce your learning with recordings or discussion. If you are a kinesthetic learner, you can ask for more action, movement, and demonstrations in the workshops you attend. You might be a learner who combines learning styles; though you have a preferred style, you can use a secondary style as well to remember more content. Trainers typically know that they should include all learning styles in their workshops, but your requests will help them be more responsive to individual differences.

> Once you have a good sense of how you learn best, seek out opportunities that make the most of your learning preferences.

To identify your learning style, answer the questions in the reproducible form "How Do You Learn Best?" on pages 155–156. In addition, many online learning style inventories can help you further identify your preferred learning style. Here are two good ones:

- Learning Style Inventory (www.personal.psu.edu/bxb11/LSI/LSI.htm)

- Index of Learning Styles Questionnaire (www.engr.ncsu.edu/learning styles/ilsweb.html)

Cultural Ways of Learning

Often, discussions about learning preferences highlight individuals. However, it's important to realize that the people around you, such as family, friends, and community members, also affect how you learn—beginning when you are very small. These influences are cultural ways of learning. Barbara Rogoff, a researcher and professor of cultural psychology, has examined how all people learn from their culture and reflect their culture in how they approach learning, problems, and living activities. Culture is around you and in you. You are constantly influenced by it. Communities and families encourage children to learn cultural practices by observing and participating in daily living, rituals, and celebrations.[6]

Your culture and upbringing may lead you to value a certain way of learning, whether it is from reading books, listening to storytelling, having hands-on experiences, or observing. So it is important to think about how your family learned together and what your community emphasized while you were growing up. Here are some questions to consider:

- Did your family value school? Education? Learning?

- Did the elders in your family pass on information through stories?

- Did your family provide opportunities for you to learn by doing?

- Think about something that a parent or another close adult in your family taught you. How did that person teach you?

- Does your family emphasize listening or speaking?

- What is conversation like in your family?

- Does your family see learning as rooted in individual or group effort?

- How do people in your family show they know or understand something?

- How do the people in your family show approval?

Paying Attention to Cultural Ways of Learning

Understanding and considering cultural ways of learning is a big part of learning to teach intentionally. Some communities have very visible cultures, partly because their practices differ from the mainstream culture. Some culture is less visible. However, we all have culture.

Because culture can be hidden to you, you may not understand how it influences you. You may think that the way your family does things is the way everyone does things. You may believe your culture is the best culture or the best way of doing things. You may misunderstand or judge others who do things differently from you. These judgments can be barriers to communication and building trust, both with your colleagues and with the families you serve.

An intentional teacher explores and values all the cultures children bring with them. He understands that unless he does this, he will not be providing optimal learning conditions for all the children. When you represent all the cultures of the children in your class, you offer opportunities to build on what they know and value. Think about the languages you use in class, the pictures you display, the books you read to the children, and the toys you include. Learn what families have in their homes, including food, eating utensils, and music. Emphasize both similarities and differences. (For example, all families eat; some families use chopsticks, while others use forks and spoons.) Think about how you communicate with children and how you expect them to communicate with you. Think about what may be familiar and unfamiliar for children in your classroom. Find ways to include families in your celebrations, crafts, and classroom activities.

You may not notice cultural learning differences until you find yourself in a situation with different cultural assumptions than you are used to. Here are several ways in which culture may affect how you approach teaching and learning:

- Some cultures emphasize learning in a group. In other cultures, elders first model how to perform a task before children are allowed to explore it. Other cultures stress independent learning.

- Some cultures acknowledge individual effort and believe this motivates children and adults. Other cultures emphasize the group's well-being and how an individual's learning contributes to the group.

▶ Some cultures require that children express themselves freely and teach children to look people in the eye as they speak as a sign of respect. In other cultures, children are taught to look down as a sign of respect and to wait until they are acknowledged before they speak.[7]

Think carefully about how you learned as a child. You can learn to communicate cross-culturally—especially if you make all your attempts with respect. But you will be most effective if you first understand how your own cultural background influences how you learn and teach.

To further explore how culture affects children and how they learn, complete the reproducible form titled "Cultural Ways of Learning" on page 157.

Once you have a good sense of how you learn best, seek out opportunities that make the most of your learning preferences. No way of learning is better than the others. They are just different. You can always try out different ways of learning, but you may want to use the style you are most comfortable with when you are learning new material or solving a big problem. When you understand how you learn, you can communicate to trainers, coaches, and supervisors what training methods work best for you.

Learning Communities or Communities of Practice

Teachers or the programs they are working in can form learning communities, or communities of practice, to explore how children learn and ways teachers can improve how they teach to engage children. Sometimes communities discuss specific children's learning topics, such as early math, literacy, or social-emotional supports. Sometimes they discuss what they have learned from data and what they want to improve. The communities share these features:

▶ a focus on learning

▶ cooperative problem solving

▶ engagement with real-life situations

▶ demonstration of strategies

▶ continuous assessment with time for reflection[8]

Learning communities or communities of practice are groups of people who learn together by focusing on common activities and goals. Through their interactions, they work to improve how they teach children. Teachers meet together to become better teachers.[9]

You can form or join a learning community or community of practice made up of individual teachers who share a common interest in improving their instruction. You and your fellow learners may or may not be coworkers. Alternatively, your employer or an organization to which you belong can also set up learning communities or communities of practice by asking teachers to meet and discuss their instructional practices.[10] Either approach can be beneficial. With such a community, you can:

- work together to solve problems
- share strategies
- explore data together
- discover what works and doesn't work
- gain more understanding of a content area
- reflect on your own growth

The emphasis should not be on perfection, but on the ways you are all learning. Learning includes mistakes. When you can share your mistakes in an open way with other teachers, it frees others to admit times when they made mistakes. Then you not only learn from your own mistakes, but from others' as well.

Teachers often develop strategies and techniques that deepen children's learning. When they share these in learning communities or communities of practice, other teachers can try them, too. For example, one teacher in our literacy project created classroom books with children. Children drew the pictures and either wrote the words with assistance or dictated their stories to the teachers. When the other teachers saw how successful this was with students and families, they tried creating books, too. In Chapter 6 you learned how one teacher, Gwen, developed routines around an estimation jar and a number line (see page 122). Other teachers in her program took her suggestions and demonstrations and made them their own.

Learning communities or communities of practice can form in many ways. Sometimes they are formal and have regularly scheduled meetings. They also can be informal, such as when teachers share strategies at the end of the day or meet to problem-solve classroom concerns.

Coaching

A coach may be called an instructional coach, a mentor, or an intervention specialist. This person provides training and support and increases the capacity of teachers to integrate math, literacy, social-emotional strategies, and other focal points into their instruction. Coaching is becoming more and more common in the early childhood field. It is another way to extend and reinforce your learning.

Coaching is provided through several avenues. Sometimes a professional development initiative hires coaches to give ongoing training and support to teachers in the project. Sometimes a program designates one person on staff to coach teachers in a variety of topics. Or, a program may hire a coach to work with beginning teachers. Teachers are sometimes asked to mentor one another in a peer-mentor arrangement.

> Working with a coach, mentor, or specialist is a give-and-take process.

If you have a coach, no matter how the relationship is set up, it gives you an opportunity to extend and deepen your learning. Some of the strategies your coach may use are as follows:

Modeling. Coaches often work with small groups of children and model learning strategies. You can watch how your coach interacts with and instructs children, even if you can't observe the whole lesson. Afterward, you can ask your coach to explain why he brought in the materials he did and how he saw children responding. You can share what you saw. The next time, you can try your coach's approach and see how it goes.

Following up training. After a training session, your coach may ask what you thought of it, if you have questions, and if you would like a few ideas to try. This follow-up helps you remember activities from the training. Ideas from training sessions are easy to forget when you are immersed in a busy classroom.

Bringing in materials. Your coach may bring in materials that align with your theme or materials that would be especially relevant for particular children in your setting. A coach often provides materials that were mentioned in training, so you can more quickly carry out your ideas.

Observing. A coach may observe your lessons, your classroom, and the children in your classroom. A coach's observations of your teaching can help you envision the specific strategies you use to promote learning and growth. She might also notice the learning needs of individual children. As she shares her observations, she helps you see yourself and your teaching from a new perspective.

Offering feedback. Your coach can offer suggestions to make a lesson more effective or discuss with you what you want to change or preserve. Your coach may offer ideas about your environment, transitions, themes, and the learning needs of children in your group. As one teacher described, "The coach observed and gave direction and advice that was personal. She was engaged. She went out of her way to find me additional resources for help."

Setting goals. A coach can help you set goals both for individual children and for your group. Not only can you set goals together, you can also brainstorm ways to reach them, based on the interests and learning styles of your students.

Assessing. A coach can help you design tools to monitor children's progress in certain content areas. Your coach may also assess children and give you a fuller picture of what they know and can do.

Working with a coach, mentor, or specialist is a give-and-take process. In the beginning of a coaching relationship, you may feel concerned about having another adult working with you and giving you feedback. (See Chapter 8 for more on this.) However, if you are able to listen constructively to feedback and share your goals for your students, you may build a relationship that enriches your teaching and contributes to your professional growth.

Sometimes you may be assigned a coach who seems distant or distracted. You may not feel that your coach is helping you learn new strategies or improve your teaching practice. First, speak with the coach about your concerns. Make sure you are specific in your feedback. For example, say it is hard if your coach is late to a scheduled observation or meeting.

Describe how that affects your planning and instruction. If your coach is moving too fast, say so—and ask to slow down a bit. If you feel that the focus is on how your coach would do things, rather than building on your strengths and supporting you through your challenges, take some time to write down a couple of concrete goals that you have in improving your teaching practice. Share the goals with your coach and ask for help in reaching these goals. This feedback may help your coach work with you more effectively. It also helps the coach become more effective overall. If you continue to be disappointed with the coaching relationship, go to a supervisor to figure out next steps. Having a coach is an opportunity for your growth that you don't want to waste.

Resources

Teachers can more quickly and effectively carry out new teaching strategies when they have resources or materials specific to the content they're learning. The math and literacy projects we conducted provided a small amount of money to classrooms so teachers could order materials and equipment to help them reach their goals. The teachers in these initiatives were enthusiastic about the materials they acquired. The materials helped them try new ideas as soon as they heard about them in the training and gave them inspiration to try new variations. Although resources are always welcome, they are most helpful if you have information from training and coaching and a framework or context within which to put the ideas.

You may be able to find resources by scrounging in dollar stores and junk shops. Or you may use your yearly allotment to order new materials that increase children's interest in a particular subject. If you have a coach, he may bring in materials to help you, such as grid and path games for early math and books and songs for literacy.

You can also use reading material in the forms of articles, books, handouts, and newsletters. These resources offer ideas, theory, and specific activities that you can adapt for the children in your setting.

The Internet is another rich source of ideas. Rachel, one of the teachers in our early math project, read about a theory called "loose parts" on a website. Architect Simon Nicholson formed this theory in 1972. He proposed that children will be more creative and inventive if given loose parts such as sand, tools, bolts, fabric, and sticks to play with in the classroom and outside on the playground. These loose parts are not to be used in a specific way; rather, children are free to combine and use the loose parts in new and interesting ways. Using this theory as a foundation, Rachel put a large tray with many items, such as natural materials (sticks, shells, acorns), construction materials (nuts, bolts, tools), and colorful toys made for counting. Rachel's students found many ways to use these loose parts for counting, sorting, combining with blocks, creating patterns, and putting together with other manipulatives. Rachel found ways to change the activity to encourage more thinking and reflection, especially around early math. Loose parts developed into a vital part of Rachel's classroom routine. (See more of Rachel's story in Chapter 9, on pages 186–188.)

Building Partnerships with Families

Including families in your journey will bring you support that you may not have expected. As a teacher, you have been trained to work with children, but you may not have equivalent training in working with families. Yet families are the lifelong teachers of their children. Families want their children to succeed, so it makes sense to engage them in the learning process.

Raising young children is a challenging task, and sometimes family members express the frustrations, anxieties, and worries that grow from this challenge when they meet with you. They may sometimes appear demanding and impatient, but in reality, they likely just don't know what to do for their child. Perhaps they are concerned about their child's readiness for kindergarten or are worried about their child's behavior at home. They may be feeling pressure or getting advice from friends and relatives about their child's progress in your classroom. If family members themselves had a difficult time in school as children, they may be afraid to engage with their child's education. They may be unsure of what to do or may fear your judgments about them.

> Families want their children to learn and be excited about learning. When you start with this assumption, you can find ways to engage families.

It is easy to misinterpret family members' comments. You may feel unsure of how to approach them. But by actively constructing partnerships with families around the needs of their children, you may find an excellent resource for support and feedback. This is especially true if you are engaging in a new initiative, learning a new curriculum, or trying a new strategy with the children. If you want to build partnerships with families around such changes, here are some helpful tips:

▶ Communicate with families about the changes you are making. Use newsletters, conferences, and casual conversations.

▶ Share your excitement about the changes you are making.

▶ Point out how the changes will benefit their children, particularly what they are learning.

▶ At your open house, offer handouts, brochures, or articles supporting your new strategies.

▶ Send home activities families can do with their children. Give specific instructions.

▶ Before you send home activities, do them with the children in your setting. This helps children know what to do, and they can show their families at home.

▶ Do assessments with the children and share the results with the families. Tell them what you are doing with the results and what they can do to help their children.

▶ Hold family events or family field trips. Use these events or outings to introduce activities related to your new initiative, such as math games or read-aloud books.

▶ Model for the families how to play the games or read the books with their children. Show families what their children are learning from doing an activity.

▶ Have conversations with families about their cultures. Reflect these cultures in your environment, your language when possible, and your activities. When you're making games or choosing books, make sure they represent the cultures in your setting.

▶ Ask families what they are seeing at home. Are their children showing excitement about what they are learning at school? Are their children eager to do the activities sent home from school? If not, what do the families suggest to engage their children?

See the reproducible form "Engaging Families" on page 158 to reflect on how you currently encourage families' participation in classroom activities. This reflection will give you ideas for strengthening your partnerships with families.

Initially, when we asked teachers to engage families in learning early math and literacy, the teachers made statements like the following:

- "They don't do the activities we send home."

- "They don't come to family events."

- "I don't know what to do to get them interested."

These statements reflected the teachers' discouragement about their connection to the families. Slowly the teachers started talking with families about their new strategies. They found families to be supportive and excited about teaching their children math and literacy. Families came to Math Nights and Book Buddies events. They not only did the activities with their children at school, they also did them at home. The families even asked teachers for more activities to do at home. One teacher reflected, "Working with the families helps us master their children's goals. We are sending activities home on Monday and getting them back on Friday. If students haven't mastered a certain skill, we work with the families to keep the activity going."

The families' responses reflect how much families really do want their children to learn and be excited about learning. If you start with this assumption, you can find ways to engage families. In our projects, sometimes the teachers tried strategies that just didn't work. Families didn't come to the family events or complete activities at home. Teachers felt discouraged, but they didn't give up. They thought about how they could change the family events or the presentation of home activities to engage families more fully. The more teachers did this, the more confident and creative they felt—and families responded enthusiastically. The families saw themselves as partners in their children's learning. One teacher recalled, "We had canvas activity bags for the kids to take home. First directions went home from the teacher, and then the kids went home and showed the families the activities. The families got excited. They saw the kids doing math."

Organizational Supports

To help teachers grow, organizations must build the infrastructure necessary to support teachers' success. Teachers can do it on their own, but when organizations prioritize teachers' professional development, they ensure more effective instruction, more satisfied teachers, and more continuity in their work with children and families. Following are some ways organizations can support teachers' growth:

Offer ongoing training. Organizations can provide ongoing training to staff rather than onetime trainings. They can make sure the trainings provide active learning and ways to explore the material with children. They can offer follow-up to the training through coaching, discussion, and materials. Many teachers learn incrementally over time. They learn specific content and strategies, then go back to the classroom and see how children are processing the activities they try. Then when teachers hear the concepts again, they understand them at a deeper level. Program administrators sometimes arrange one-day workshops and expect teachers to implement the changes right away. That isn't a realistic approach. Instructional change takes time, repetition, and feedback. Ongoing training is a powerful tool, especially when training is offered consistently throughout the year.

Make time. Time is always at a premium in early childhood settings. By setting aside time for training, discussion, planning, and assessment, organizations demonstrate that teacher development is a priority.

Provide opportunities to meet. Teachers need opportunities to meet with their coaches and other teachers in order to form the learning communities or communities of practice that are so valuable to their continued professional development. This issue is closely related to making the time to meet, but it is also about providing a place for meetings, reading materials, and leadership to keep meetings focused on teaching and instruction. Regular meetings help teachers learn to use their time together to focus on issues directly related to teaching young children.

Find money for professional development. Early childhood programs are usually strapped for cash. But even if a program cannot provide a large infusion of cash, arranging the budget to provide resources for training, materials, curriculum, and assessment demonstrates the program's commitment to each teacher's development. Investment in teachers' development brings rewards for children.

Structure ways to collect and analyze data. Teachers become more intentional when they can connect data to their strategies. When teachers implement their lessons and see the children's assessments afterward, teachers find it easier to reflect on their instruction. Even when programs provide ways to collect data through an assessment system, teachers may not see the results in time to analyze and plan from them. Or they may have only individual results for the children in their class, not group results. Teachers need to see both, preferably through charts, graphs, and other organized data. And teachers analyze better if they can look at results together and discuss what brought about the results. An assessment and analysis structure may be hard to set up at first, and teachers may resist it. It is important to communicate to teachers that this is a learning opportunity, not a punishment. Once it is a routine, teachers will value the information.

Suggest ways to connect to families. Children do better when their families are involved in their education. Teachers sometimes get discouraged when families don't respond to their overtures. Programs can help provide the necessary bridge between families and children by publishing newsletters, establishing lending libraries, planning field trips, and creating bulletin boards that reinforce the concepts teachers are exploring with the children.

At the beginning of this chapter, you read about Chantelle's dilemma. Chantelle wanted to involve her fellow teachers in providing early literacy experiences for the children in their program. She wanted to build a learning community where all the teachers could share what was working for them and what they wanted to improve. However, Chantelle found her presentations on early literacy to the rest of the staff were not helping them carry out the strategies. She was disappointed at her fellow teachers' lack of enthusiasm and decided to meet with the director. Together, Chantelle and the director came up with a plan. The director knew this early literacy initiative could help all the program's teachers become more effective and intentional. So she scheduled ongoing training and set aside time each month for the teachers to meet and discuss the trainings and the early literacy activities teachers were doing in their classrooms. She observed each teacher once a month and met with the teachers to reflect on their work with children. Because the program's budget was tight, the director applied for a grant to buy more books and literacy materials. Chantelle was relieved she had met with the director, and she supported the director's efforts. She was excited to be part of a community focused on children and how they learn.

Advocating for Organizational Support

When teachers don't have adequate organizational supports, such as training, planning time, breaks, and effective ratios, this affects the whole organization, including children, parents, and other teachers. If you feel a need for more organizational supports, approach this need as an opportunity for your organization, school, or program to improve. Think about it as a problem to solve for the good of everyone. This means you have a role in helping solve the problem.

Before you approach your supervisor or director, take some time to identify the problem. If possible, write a description of the problem in clear language. Answer the following question: What organizational supports do you feel you need? Next, build a case for why developing those supports would benefit the organization. Think about possible solutions given the realities of your own organization. For example, if you are finding you have no time to talk with your teaching team or other teachers about training or using new strategies, planning, and assessment, think about how you might find that time. Finding time may require making tradeoffs; for example, taking turns covering naptime so half the team can meet during that time, or freeing time by replacing meetings focused on announcements with written communications about the same information, requiring everyone to read and sign off. Or if your organization is short of funds for training, think about how you could find more money to use. You could apply for scholarships provided by sponsoring organizations. You could raise funds specifically allotted to training for the staff.

Approach your supervisor or director not as a complainer but as a problem solver. Indicate your willingness to work together. Assume you are both invested in improving your program. Try to schedule a specific meeting to speak with your supervisor or director. If you present your thinking and some of what you have written down, your supervisor or director will know you are serious about working together.

You might feel a little helpless if your organization has problems. You may not feel you can influence those who are making decisions. You may not want to be a troublemaker. However, there are many ways you can contribute to finding solutions. Here are some of them:

- **Brainstorm possible solutions.** For example, team up with a small group of staff and parents to come up with new approaches to parent involvement.

- **Rethink schedules.** For example, take turns participating in online training during naptime.

- **Strategize ways to exchange responsibilities or let some other things go.** For example, ask if another teacher can lead group time while you help a colleague learn a new online assessment system.
- **Volunteer to facilitate teacher sharing.** For example, lead a discussion on an article the staff has read or share a successful strategy you have learned in a workshop.

Finding support on your teaching journey is crucial to maintaining your growth. When you begin instructional change, you may be very enthusiastic, but as time goes on, you may find it harder to continue your efforts on a daily basis. It is easy to get worn down by the constant demands on your energy. You can find support from other teachers, both within your program and in the community, from your program administrators and supervisors, from the families in your program, and from the children themselves. To identify the supports you have as a teacher and to figure out where you could build more support, fill out the reproducible form "Circles of Support" on pages 159–160.

Your growth as a teacher will not always be easy or straightforward. You will need inspiration, encouragement, and feedback. With these supports, you will find a way around the detours to keep moving forward.

References

1. Susan M. Sheridan, Carolyn Pope Edwards, Christin A. Marvin, and Lisa L. Knoche, "Professional Development in Early Childhood Classrooms: Process Issues and Research Needs," *Early Education and Development* 20, no. 3 (2009): 377–401.

2. Ravay Snow-Renner and Patricia A. Lauer, *McRel Insights: Professional Development Analysis* (Denver: McRel, 2005): 6. files.eric.ed.gov/fulltext/ED491305.pdf.

3. Alma Fleet and Catherine Patterson, "Professional Growth Reconceptualized: Early Childhood Staff Searching for Meaning," *Early Childhood Research and Practice* 3, no. 2 (Fall 2001), ecrp.uiuc.edu/v3n2/fleet.html.

4. David Riley and Mary A. Roach, "Helping Teachers Grow: Toward Theory and Practice of an 'Emergent Curriculum' Model of Staff Development," *Early Childhood Education Journal* 33, no. 5 (2006): 363–370.

5. Catherine Whitehead, "Definition of Learning Style," eHow, accessed September 17, 2015, www.ehow.com /about_6551473_definition-learning-style.html.

6. Barbara Rogoff, *Developing Destinies: A Mayan Midwife and Town* (New York: Oxford University Press, 2011): 257.

7. Louise Derman-Sparks and Julie Olsen Edwards. *Anti-Bias Education for Young Children and Ourselves* (Washington, DC: NAEYC, 2010): 56–60.

8. Violet H. Harada, Debora Lum, and Kathy Souza. "Building a Learning Community: Students and Adults as Inquirers," *Childhood Education* (Winter 2002–2003): 68–71.

9. Judy Harris Helm, "Building Communities of Practice," *Young Children* 62, no. 4 (2007): 12–16.

10. Ibid.

Training Preferences

How teacher training is structured affects your ability to learn. Review this list to begin understanding what types of training will help you succeed as a learner. What's the right mix for you?

Training Method	I Prefer This Training Method (Yes, No, Sometimes)	Why?	Drawbacks to This Method
Time to exchange ideas			
Feedback			
Listening to lectures or experts			
Watching videos			
Online learning			

Training Method	I Prefer This Training Method (Yes, No, Sometimes)	Why?	Drawbacks to This Method
Reading materials and research			
Hands-on practice			
Small group			
Large group			

Do you have any preferences for timing, duration, frequency, or day of the week? What are they?

What's missing that, if present, would enhance your learning?

Once you have completed this form, keep it handy. Pull it out so you can compare training opportunities to achieve your learning objectives.

How Do You Learn Best?

Think about the following questions. Your answer may not be a simple yes or no. Describe why you answered the way you did. More detail will help you understand your learning style better.

Do you retain information you hear on the radio better than what you read?

When you are hearing a lecture, do you want a picture, chart, video, or handout to help you process the information?

Are you often restless when you're listening to a speaker? Do you find that you want to be doing something?

Do you remember activities better when you have already done them ahead of time or soon after a training?

Do you take notes to help you remember?

Do you learn better when lessons include music or other sounds?

What did you notice about yourself as you filled out this short survey?

Describe how you would like to try learning new material in the future. What learning methods would you use?

If you prefer visual aids or like to take notes to remember material, you prefer the **VISUAL** learning style.

If you learn better with music or sound or by hearing information, you prefer the **AUDITORY** learning style.

If you want to be moving and you remember training better if you have done the activities, you prefer the **KINESTHETIC** learning style.

Sometimes **COMBINING LEARNING METHODS** can strengthen your memory.

Cultural Ways of Learning

In the center of this form, describe a concept you want children in your group to learn or explore. Pick at least three "bubbles," and in them, describe three different ways children might explore or learn the concept you've described. The blank bubble is a space for you to add another cultural way of learning that you've observed in the children or their families.

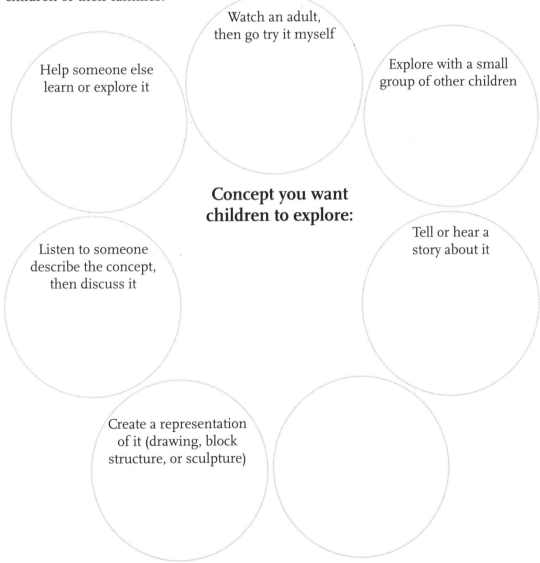

Watch an adult, then go try it myself

Help someone else learn or explore it

Explore with a small group of other children

Concept you want children to explore:

Listen to someone describe the concept, then discuss it

Tell or hear a story about it

Create a representation of it (drawing, block structure, or sculpture)

Engaging Families

How do you engage parents in their children's learning?

Evaluate how your outreach to parents is going. What is working well? What needs improvement?

What would you like to add or change to increase the participation of families?

How do you reflect the cultures of families in your classroom?

Circles of Support

We all do better when we have support to grow as professionals. Take a moment to reflect on your supports. Work your way through the Circle of Support below and write down examples of each type of support.

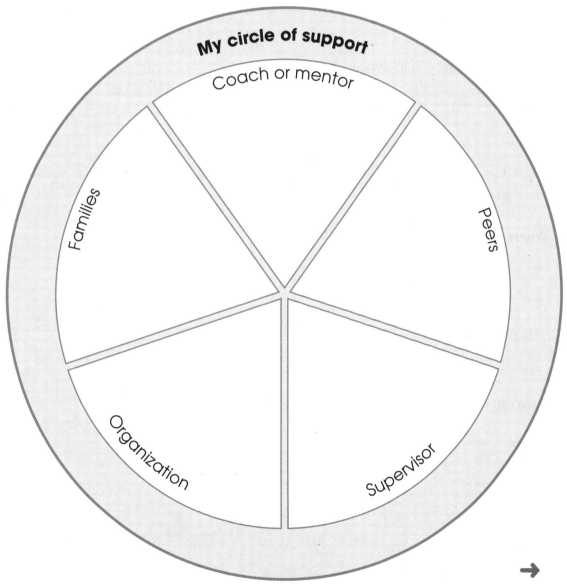

Reflect on your supports by answering the following questions:

What do you notice?

Where do you feel you have enough support?

Where could you use more support?

How can you get the additional support you need?

8 NAVIGATING THE DETOURS ON THE JOURNEY

Jamie was a new employee; he had just begun teaching the three-year-old class. He had twenty children and two assistant teachers. His director had just told him their program would be applying for a rating in the state Quality Rating and Improvement System (QRIS). As part of that effort, Jamie would need to be observed in the classroom, do more paperwork, and have a coach. Although he nodded his head, he really didn't understand what all this meant. But he didn't want to ask any questions for fear the director would think he wasn't competent enough to be teaching. He asked a couple of the other teachers in the program about QRIS, but they just shrugged their shoulders and shook their heads. He wasn't sure where he should go next to find out more about the process. Jamie's discomfort was compounded by the fact that he was new. And the other teachers in his program seemed confused and resentful—which worried Jamie even more.

Jamie's experience is not unusual. Often, teachers are told what will be happening but are given no details or explanations. Supporting teachers' professional development requires thought and planning, creativity and flexibility. Many organizations have a vision of investing in their teachers in this way, but limited money, time, and personnel often shape their reality.

Jamie felt overwhelmed by this new QRIS demand. He needed more support. But he wasn't sure how he could get it. For Jamie, this problem was a detour on his journey. He was ready to begin teaching his class, getting to know his students and their families, and setting his classroom routines. Now he had another issue to deal with.

Detours like Jamie's can feel overwhelming—but they aren't impossible to navigate. Doing so requires defining the problem, outlining possible

161

options, and deciding on a course of action. It requires both teachers' and supervisors' participation. When you're facing a detour, it may take several tries to find the problem-solving approach that works in your organization. If your first attempt doesn't work, remember that it is a start. Every effort you make gets you closer to finding the information and support you need to get back on track.

This chapter will first discuss the problem-solving process. Next, it'll explore specific problems and concerns we have heard from teachers and administrators.

How Do You Approach a Problem?

You probably have a typical or preferred way of dealing with problems. How you approach a problem depends on your personality, your childhood experiences, what has worked for you in the past, your comfort with conflict, and your ability to keep trying. Your approach could depend on the problem, too. For example, some people can easily problem-solve technological issues but are reluctant to bring up concerns with team members.

> Always using the same approaches, especially if they aren't working for you, may hinder effective problem solving and increase frustration.

Think about how you approach problems or conflicts with others:

- Do you avoid conflict at all costs?
- Do you tend to approach a conflict in anger?
- Do you blame yourself when something goes wrong?
- Do you tend to blame others when things go wrong?
- Do you become discouraged and give up easily?
- Do you keep trying until you find a solution?
- Do you try to understand the problem before trying to solve it?

These are all ways of approaching problems. Some of them probably don't work very well for you. Others you may use over and over again. Most people tend to fall back on the same approaches when they encounter problems.

Sophie, a first-grade teacher, had a conflict with the teacher in the room next door. The neighboring teacher was older and more experienced and was always coming into Sophie's room to offer suggestions about room arrangement, bulletin boards, and activities. These visits were getting on Sophie's nerves, but she was very uncomfortable with conflict and said nothing for a while. She usually left problems alone just to see if they would resolve themselves. However, she eventually realized that the problem was not going away. It actually seemed to be getting worse. Sophie decided to change her approach. She tried to understand what her colleague might be feeling. She spoke with the neighboring teacher directly about how uncomfortable the visits made her. After the conversation, her colleague stayed away for a while. But eventually they were able to share ideas that increased both teachers' skills.

Always using the same approaches, especially if they aren't working for you, may hinder effective problem solving and increase frustration. For example, if you are feeling overwhelmed in your work, it may seem easiest to blame yourself or others for the problem. But both of these approaches can block actual problem solving. Emotions can get tangled into the conflict and keep you from seeing a way forward.

Fill out the reproducible form "How Do You Approach a Problem?" on pages 176–177 to examine your usual way of approaching problems. This form can help you monitor your habits, evaluate whether they're effective, and learn new ways of addressing problems.

Effective Problem Solving: A Seven-Step Process

Trying to solve a problem too quickly may result in wasted effort. Effective problem solving requires time, thought, and patience. You are likely to reach a better conclusion by using the seven-step process presented in the "Seven-Step Problem Solving" chart on the next page.

This problem-solving process looks straightforward and easy to carry out, but you may find it more difficult when you actually put it in to practice. Let's use Jamie's story to see how the seven steps work.

In the story at the beginning of this chapter, Jamie was a new teacher in a center just starting the QRIS process. He didn't know what this process meant for him or his classroom. He had recently gone to a training

Seven-Step Problem Solving*

Problem-Solving Step	Explanation
1. Identify the problem.	After looking at the problem and other issues that may be surrounding it, focus on the main problem. Sometimes this focus is difficult because the surrounding issues are so big.
2. Gather information.	Find out what happened before and after the problem occurred. Seek information about others' experiences with the problem.
3. Brainstorm solutions.	Write down all the possible solutions, even if they seem far-fetched. Allowing far-fetched ideas can spark more creativity. Try not to censor yourself or others.
4. Pick the best idea.	Choose the idea most likely to work and be implemented. Consider what you can realistically do. Look at your time, your abilities, and your experience.
5. Try it.	Try your idea. Don't give up quickly if it is not working at first. Give it two or three weeks.
6. Decide if it is working.	After you have given your idea a chance to work, decide if it is indeed working. If the problem has resolved or is happening less, you are on the right track.
7. Revise your approach if needed.	If you decide your idea is not working, choose another idea to try, or change your plan a little. Remember that an idea that doesn't work is not a failure. It gives you valuable information for your next attempt.

*When Play Isn't Fun: Helping Children Resolve Play Conflicts by Sandra Heidemann and Deborah Hewitt. Copyright © 2014 by Sandra Heidemann and Deborah Hewitt. Reprinted by permission of Redleaf Press, Saint Paul, MN, www.redleafpress.org.

on problem solving, so he decided to use a worksheet he had gotten there to help him tackle this problem. Here's how he followed the seven-step process:

1. **Identify the problem.** Jamie knew he felt overwhelmed, but he wasn't sure what was more overwhelming: the QRIS project or the fact that he was new. He wrote down his concerns:

   ▶ I am new in the program.

   ▶ I have a new class.

   ▶ I have a new curriculum to learn.

▶ I was told I would have to participate in the QRIS project this year.

▶ I don't know what the QRIS project means for me.

He decided his main problem was finding out what the QRIS project meant for him in the coming year. Other issues were pressing as well, but he had a better idea of where to go with those.

2. **Gather information.** Jamie had already found out that at least two of the teachers seemed as confused as he was about the QRIS project. He searched the Internet to find out more about QRIS generally. He looked at the center for any brochures or handouts being distributed to families but didn't find any. He spoke with a couple of friends from school who were teaching in child care centers.

3. **Brainstorm solutions.** Jamie made a list of possible solutions to finding out what the QRIS project meant for him. As he was making the list, he tried not to focus on the reasons why his ideas might not work.

   ▶ Research QRIS on the Internet some more.

   ▶ Talk to other teachers in my program.

   ▶ Talk again with my friends in other programs.

   ▶ Talk with the director.

4. **Pick the best idea.** Jamie looked at each of his ideas and chose to speak with the director about the QRIS project and what it meant for him. He thought she probably had the most information about what it would mean at his center, and all his other ideas were either too general or were problematic. Talking to the other teachers in his center might only stir up dissatisfaction with the director, and he wanted to get started on the right foot with her. He was worried about looking negative or incompetent to her, but he decided that talking with the director was still his best idea.

5. **Try it.** Jamie did go in to speak with his director. He prepared a list of questions he could refer to if needed. Although she was able to answer some of his questions, she needed more information, too. She had signed up for QRIS because parents were asking about it, and she thought it could be a good professional development opportunity.

However, she was still learning about it. Like the teachers, she had many questions.

6. **Decide if it is working.** Both Jamie and the director were glad they had met. However, they both still had a lot of unanswered questions and needed more information. When Jamie told her that a couple of other staff members seemed confused as well, the director was concerned.

7. **Revise your approach if needed.** Together Jamie and the director decided to bring his questions and concerns to the whole staff. The director thought other teachers might be feeling some of the same anxiety as Jamie, and as a group they could discuss the issue.

Jamie shared his problem-solving worksheet with the director, and she decided to use the same process with the staff when they discussed the QRIS process. Here's how the group followed the seven-step process:

1. **Identify the problem.** The director described why she had made the decision to sign up for the QRIS project. She also said that she wondered whether teachers were feeling anxious and unsure about what the project meant for them. She asked teachers to list their concerns and also identify what they thought the main problem was. The teachers listed:

   ▶ This is too much to do.

   ▶ I'm not sure about having a coach.

   ▶ Will we have to start using another curriculum?

   ▶ What if we get a low rating?

   ▶ How are ratings decided?

   ▶ I don't really know what this means for me, my workload, and my stress.

   After a rich discussion, the group decided that the main problem was that the teachers and director didn't really know what the QRIS process meant for them.

2. **Gather information.** Teachers shared what they had heard about the QRIS process. Jamie passed around information he had gotten from the Internet. The group quickly realized they didn't have all the same

information. Some of it sounded like rumors, but the group didn't really know for sure.

3. **Brainstorm solutions.** Together, the group members listed ways they could get more information:

   ▶ Research QRIS on their state website.

   ▶ List all their questions in one place.

   ▶ Contact the lead agency for QRIS and ask their questions.

   ▶ Contact the person in charge of QRIS for the center and ask that person to come to a staff meeting to talk about it.

   ▶ See if they had a coach assigned and ask the coach to visit.

   ▶ Talk to staff in other child care centers who had gone through the QRIS process.

4. **Pick the best idea.** The group looked at all the ideas and decided it would work best if they contacted the person in charge of QRIS for the center and ask that person to come to a staff meeting. That way everyone would hear the same information, and they could ask their questions directly. If that person couldn't come, maybe a representative could.

5. **Try it.** They invited the person in charge of QRIS for the center. He came and answered as many questions as he could. He said that although the process was somewhat defined, officials were still making decisions about what would happen in the next year.

6. **Decide if it is working.** The staff members were relieved to hear the same information and get answers to some of their questions. But they were also left with many questions, particularly about what the QRIS process would mean for them.

7. **Revise your approach if needed.** The staff decided to invite staff from another child care center to discuss how the QRIS process unfolded there. The director also pledged she would leave time in each staff meeting to discuss the QRIS process. If more questions arose, she would do her best to find the answers.

What started out as Jamie's private concern became a springboard for addressing the concerns of the whole staff. The staff felt included and respected because they were involved in working out solutions. When they finished the seven-step process, the director and the staff members all felt more positive and upbeat about resolving their problem.

The seven-step approach may seem cumbersome and time-consuming at first, but when you use it frequently, it becomes second nature. You can use this process to solve problems with colleagues, with your organizational management, and even with the children in your class. Teaching children to use this approach empowers them to solve conflicts themselves, even if you aren't within reach. When you want to try this problem-solving approach, use the reproducible form titled "Problem-Solving Worksheet" on pages 178–179.

Problem Solving and Professional Development: Questions and Concerns

Understanding the implementation of QRIS was a professional development issue for Jamie, the other teachers, and their director. Many different professional development concerns can arise for early childhood teachers, and some questions come up frequently. Following are many of the common questions we have heard over the years and strategies to address them. You may also come up with your own creative and workable solutions.

> Problems do not have to overwhelm us. They are opportunities to become more innovative thinkers and doers.

Bench Strength
What if coaching is not available?
Coaching is a valuable tool for teachers as they learn new content and unfamiliar strategies. However, it may not be possible to add a full-time coaching position to support teachers. Here are some ideas from programs that have found ways to offer some coaching despite financial challenges:

▶ Find funds for a part-time coach. Sometimes coaching responsibilities can be combined with a teacher's or manager's responsibilities.

▶ Ask a supervisor knowledgeable about early childhood to provide coaching, observations, and feedback.

▶ Set up peer-mentoring relationships, so you and your fellow teachers can coach one another.

▶ Share a coach with another program or two. Perhaps another program near you could use a coach.

▶ Sign up for a professional development initiative that includes coaching.

Time Crunch

What if there is not enough time for professional development?
The most pressing issue teachers tell us they face is lack of time. Perhaps, like some teachers, you can't even think about adding more content to your day. Maybe you feel you have no time to go to trainings or meetings. Or maybe you cannot find time to plan, make materials, or do research into new strategies. This problem has no single solution. Here are some suggestions:

▶ **No time to meet.** Ask your supervisor to provide substitute teachers when possible so you are free to plan and meet with other teachers or with your coach. You need time to reflect on how your strategies are working with your students and what kinds of progress they are making.

▶ **No time in the schedule to add new content.** Find ways to infuse your daily routines with early math, science, and literacy. Work on social-emotional skills not only during group time, but also at other times, such as during dramatic play and outside time. Use all the time you have with children to keep them engaged in purposeful learning. (Hint: the more comfortable you become with new content, the easier it becomes to integrate that content into routines and other learning experiences.)

▶ **No time for training.** Some programs close periodically for staff professional development days. These days offer staff an opportunity to learn what other teachers are doing, gain more training, attend conferences, and find materials. If your program does not offer such opportunities, look carefully at your tasks to see if you can let go of some to free up time for professional development.

Tight Budget

My program has no money for materials or trainings.

If your program has no extra money in the budget for staff development or equipment, plan to scrounge for materials. Search rummage sales or garage sales for old cash registers, keyboards, and used toys. Go to dollar stores and secondhand stores for cheap math counters and used books. Talk with your supervisor about approaching local businesses or charitable organizations, such as service groups, foundations, book clubs, and religious organizations, which might be willing to donate materials or money toward classroom materials. If you solicit donations, be sure you provide criteria or reserve the right of refusal, because not everything people want to donate will be appropriate. One program we worked with received a generous donation of books to use with the children. However, the books had too many words on each page, and the concepts were too complicated for young children. Helping organizations understand what kinds of books, games, and toys are suitable for young children will ensure more success.

Your director may be able to find trainers willing to work for a sliding-scale fee. Ask your fellow teachers if they would be willing to lead workshops for your colleagues. Plan to present something you are excited about. Even short presentations can help teachers think up new and creative ideas. To gather more ideas, go to a used bookstore and see if it has curriculum books for sale. Use the Internet to brainstorm ideas. Many early childhood education websites offer creative ideas and templates for activities and discussion. Some early childhood organizations' websites offer free online trainings. You can also find many excellent videos of child development experts speaking on a variety of topics. Use your Internet smarts and be sure to choose reputable organizations as sources.

Resistance to Change

I have asked my director for more information about early math and early literacy, but she said we don't have time this year to do more training. She thinks we have done well so far and don't need to change. I would like to push myself to become a better teacher. How can I move myself forward? How can I get my director interested in this?

Your director may just feel good about her program and not want to disturb what seems to be working well. Or perhaps she's uncomfortable with change. As we have discussed at some length in this book, change can be stressful—even when it's positive. Sometimes directors hold core beliefs that require rethinking and redefining. (See Chapter 1.) The changes you would like to make are probably aligned with your director's philosophy, but she may not realize it. You could invite her interest in the following ways:

- Occasionally give her articles about the kinds of progress young children make when given opportunities to learn early math and literacy.

- Share information about how appropriate early childhood math and literacy education benefits young children and can close the achievement gap.

- Suggest ways to market early literacy and math training and coaching to families.

- Sign up for classes and share what you learn with your director.

- Offer to help her carry out changes in the curriculum, environment, or program.

- Ask your director to watch you use a new strategy in your classroom, so she can see it in action. Share your own learning experience, and note children's positive responses as concretely as possible. Be sure you've already introduced and used this strategy successfully before having your director watch.

If you find your overtures aren't working, and your director is still reluctant to make changes, plan to make changes in your teaching on your own. Find other teachers who are interested in this change either in your own program or in other early childhood programs. Take classes and work to implement the suggestions and activities you learn. When your director sees how children and families are responding, she may change her mind and embrace these new ideas. Remember this bit of advice from educator and author Joseph Bruchac: "The best teachers have showed me that things have to be done bit by bit. Nothing that means anything happens quickly—we only think it does."[1]

Judgment Jitters

My program just joined an early literacy project, and as part of that, I am going to have a literacy coach. I am a little nervous, and I am not sure what it will be like. I don't want my coach to judge how I teach. How can I calm my nerves?

Most teachers are a little nervous about having a coach. You don't want to be judged, and you probably are a little afraid that you might be doing things wrong. Add some possible embarrassment about the reality that things rarely go smoothly in an early childhood classroom, and it is completely understandable that you would worry about having another person in your room.

However, having a coach can be an opportunity to explore a whole new area of instruction. The coach can be an ally who helps you reflect and grow. Here are some suggestions to help you move through this transition:

▶ Schedule regular meetings with your coach, and try to keep that schedule. It will be easier to have a trusting relationship with your coach if you meet often, even if the meetings are short.

▶ If you prefer or benefit more from certain forms of communication, discuss those with your coach. For example, some teachers prefer seeing written feedback in advance; others prefer a phone conversation or texting. For ongoing communication and coordination, some teachers like to touch base with their coaches in person. Other teachers are most comfortable with informal communications via email. Whatever forms of communication you prefer, be sure to agree on a plan for how you will communicate with your coach.

▶ Your coach will have subject areas to talk about, such as trainings you have been to, what you would like to learn about, and questions you may have. Share your thoughts and questions with your coach. Before you meet, think about what you might like to learn or practice. Set goals and possible strategies together. This is *your* learning, and it is important that you own it.

▶ If you have questions about a technique your coach is suggesting, ask for a demonstration. If the coach is offering suggestions on your environment, ask for help in rearranging it. Sometimes it is easier to understand a strategy if you see it.

 ▶ If you are trying a strategy and it doesn't seem to be working, ask your coach for feedback. Sometimes a simple change can make a strategy more successful. One coach added a number line to an estimation activity and observed that the children were then able to learn numbers more easily.

 ▶ If you have a strategy that is working, share your excitement with your coach. Your coach will be as excited as you are. Ask your coach to observe the strategy and offer feedback.

 ▶ Although you can improve your teaching on your own, you will go further faster with a coach. It takes time to build a trusting coaching relationship, but the extra time is a worthwhile investment in the long run.

Overbooked

I would like to have a learning community (see Chapter 7) with other teachers in my program, but they all say they are too busy and don't want to do it right now. How can I generate interest and get something going? Teachers are always too busy, and they don't always recognize the benefits they can gain from a learning community or community of practice. Try to start very small. Ask your director or supervisor if teachers can have just a small portion of your staff meeting to share successful techniques, transitions, or strategies with one another. Make sure everyone gets a turn, but don't force anyone to share.

Ask if you can meet with other teachers to look at your students' assessment results or work samples. Although teachers may not want to share the data with other teachers, they may be open to sharing strategies and identifying what they think makes a difference.

Invite other staff to go to a workshop with you and talk about what you learned afterward. Your colleagues may not want to do this, but if they do, you have started to build a learning community together.

It is important to remain accepting of how other teachers wish to participate. If teachers feel judged or manipulated, they will shut down communication. Be positive and supportive toward your colleagues.

If your coworkers are not responsive to your efforts, go outside the circle of your program and find other teachers with whom you might build a professional learning community. For example, you might choose to join an online community.

Gaming for Change

I really want to try some new games I've learned with the children in my classroom to help them develop their numeracy, literacy, and social-emotional skills, but I am afraid of expecting too much of them and giving them anxiety about learning. I have been warned about drilling children, and I don't want to do that. How can I challenge my students a bit more without making them anxious?

It's true: drilling children can give them anxiety, especially if they aren't picking up the information quickly. But playing games isn't the same as drilling children. Children love playing games and will learn to count and recognize numerals and letters, as well as practice social-emotional skills, through game playing. Games engage children and make learning fun.

The field of early childhood is changing. For many years, teachers used games to teach and reinforce social skills but resisted doing math and literacy activities with young children, fearing exactly what's expressed in this section's question. But it is possible to teach math and literacy in a developmentally appropriate way. Exposing children to learning numbers and letters opens up their worlds and helps them get ready for the next steps in their education. It may also close the opportunity gap many children from low-income families experience. If you try math and literacy games, you may find that children respond enthusiastically. They may ask to play the games often and may ask you for more games. Their eager responses will support your decision to add games to your setting.

Families as Partners

The parents in my program don't seem to be interested in what I am doing with their children. They are too busy. They don't send back the activities I send home for them to do with their children. What can I do to communicate with parents and encourage them to be more engaged?

Parents and other family members generally do want their young children to succeed and are invested in seeing their preschool children reach kindergarten ready to participate. Families anxiously await word from teachers that their children are doing well. However, families may not always respond to your overtures as a teacher for several reasons:

- They may simply be too busy with multiple jobs or may have several children in different schools.

- They may feel intimidated by school, based on their own experiences as children.

- They may believe that teaching is a teacher's job.

- They may feel incompetent to teach their children.

- They may worry that you will judge them if they do things "wrong."

On the flip side, it's easy for us as teachers to focus solely on what we want children to learn. Sometimes we feel too busy or distracted to experiment with ways to engage families in the learning process.

Think about easy, fun learning activities families can do with their children. Invite them to family events focused on fun ways to learn. Stay positive and respectful. You may find parents and other family members responding more enthusiastically than you expect. As one teacher commented after reaching out to families, "Parents will now say they can't come into the classroom, but they go on to ask what they can do at home to help—I have seen a big increase in that." (See Chapter 7 for more ideas on engaging families.)

Remember: your growth as a teacher will not always be easy or straightforward. Part of being a more intentional teacher is learning to solve the problems you encounter. The solutions you try may not be perfect. But if you keep trying when the first idea doesn't work, you learn how to persevere and become more confident in your problem-solving abilities. Effective problem solving also requires creativity. By coming up with interesting ideas, you communicate to your colleagues and the children in your class that it's always possible to find positive solutions. Problems do not have to overwhelm us. They are opportunities to become more innovative thinkers and doers.

References

1. Alan Kaufman, *Our Identities: Multicultural Readings for Writers* (Dubuque, IA: Kendall/Hunt Publishing Company, 1994): 60.

How Do You Approach a Problem?

For each of the following scenarios, check the response that you are most likely to make.

	Like Me	Somewhat Like Me	Not Like Me at All
1. When I notice that coworkers are having problems, I ask them about it.			
2. When I disagree with colleagues, I tell them.			
3. When I am angry or upset, I blow up at my team members.			
4. When my team decides how to handle something in the classroom and I disagree, I go along so I won't upset anyone.			
5. If I am having a problem with my director or a coworker, I ignore it, hoping it will go away.			
6. My family handles conflict by discussing it.			

What can you learn from your responses? What do you notice about how you handle conflict and problems?

Do you notice differences in how you respond depending on who you're in conflict with? Explain.

What approach do you feel works best for you? Why?

What would you like to change?

Problem-Solving Worksheet

1. Identify the problem:

2. Gather information:

3. Brainstorm solutions:

4. Pick the best idea:

5. Try it:

6. Decide if it is working:

7. Revise your approach if needed:

9 REFLECTING ON YOUR JOURNEY

In this book, you have explored the many forces that steer your journey as a teacher. You started by looking at how you began your career, what you believe about how children and adults learn, what you value as a teacher, and what your purpose is. You've thought about how you have changed as you've gained experience and knowledge. You've explored the relationship between change and increasing your purposeful instruction. You've examined the many changes you have been asked to make.

You've learned about the three phases of growth: Teachers Learn, Teachers Practice, and Teachers Share and Model. Hopefully, by understanding these three phases, you'll be able to have patience with yourself as you learn new content and techniques. You've delved into the supports you need on your teaching journey, such as training, learning communities or communities of practice, coaching, and resources, and you've gotten suggestions for solving problems that may arise. You have traced your journey from your first steps as a teacher to your passages through changes and challenges to the spot where you stand today.

Each journey is unique. Although teachers may have some similar experiences, your journey has had its own twists and turns. More than likely, you've had many surprises along the way.

The following picture shows the journey of a teacher named Jeanne. We offer Jeanne's journey as just one example. Your journey may look very different from hers.

Jeanne's Journey

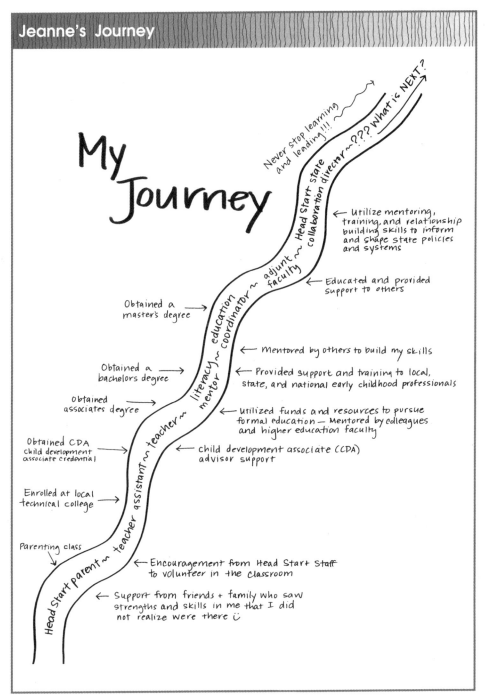

Reprinted with permission of Jeanne Dickhausen.

Jeanne's journey began when her daughter was a young student in Head Start. As you look at Jeanne's journey, you can see that she moved from being a parent to being an aide to being a teacher to being a coach to being an early childhood specialist working for the state. She doesn't know what will come next, but she thinks that is the most interesting part of plotting her journey. She does know where she has been, and she can use what she has learned through her career to help her find her way forward.[1]

Looking at where you have been and where you would like to go can give you a new perspective on your own journey. Turn to page 191 at the end of this chapter, where you'll find a reproducible form titled "My Journey." Take a little time to write and reflect on the road you have taken by filling out this worksheet.

Cycle of Continuous Improvement

As you reflect on your journey, you may note how often you sought to improve in your work with children and families. You can think about

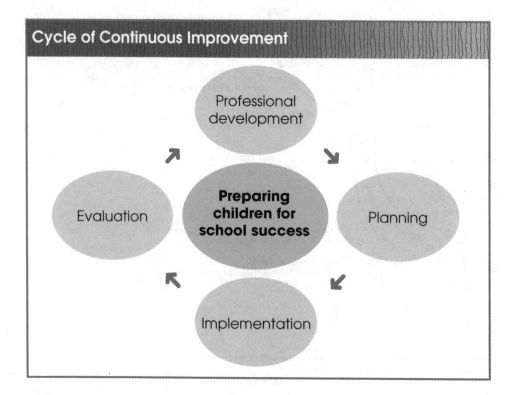

Cycle of Continuous Improvement

Professional development

Preparing children for school success

Planning

Evaluation

Implementation

this ongoing growth using a framework called the cycle of continuous improvement. This framework describes the process you experience as you teach day by day. The four tasks in the cycle—professional development, planning, implementation, and evaluation—are central to increasing your knowledge, skill, and purposeful instruction. You perform these tasks continually both as you teach individual lessons on a daily basis and as you work toward your longer-term monthly or yearly goals. The cycle doesn't really start at one task and end at another. Each task forms the launchpad for the next step.

Professional Development

You receive professional development, or learn new content and strategies, through your workplace, through colleges and universities, and through your own explorations by reading and attending workshops and conferences. Coaching and mentoring deepen your learning. From this professional development, you gain new understanding from research and new ideas for strategies. Using this information, your observations, and previous knowledge, you set the stage for planning.

Planning

Planning in a thoughtful and deliberate way requires attention to details and competing priorities. Choosing your direction means setting goals—both short-term and long-term ones. Teachers often struggle with defining specific, measurable goals. It is much easier to simply find strategies and activities that engage children. But children will learn more if you base your choices of strategies and activities on the goals you have set, rather than choosing strategies based solely on what children enjoy.

After you set your goals, find engaging and effective strategies to reach those goals. You will find strategies in books, online, and from other teachers. Next, it is time to implement these strategies.

Planning Considerations

Here are some factors to consider as you plan your goals and lesson plans:

- your knowledge of the content area

- your observations of the children in your class

- your evaluation of their skills

- your knowledge of child development

- what will engage your students

- your knowledge of early learning standards

Implementation

As you implement your strategies, you find that sometimes they work well and sometimes they don't. You will need to tweak your strategies even as you teach. You will need to decide when to repeat lessons and when to change them.

Evaluation

Evaluation is the last step in the cycle of continuous improvement. It happens as you teach, after the lesson, and much later, when you see how children are meeting your long-term goals. Here are some questions to ask yourself as you evaluate your instruction:

▶ Were the children engaged in the activities?

▶ Did the activities work for all the children?

▶ Did you prepare adequately for the activity?

▶ What would you change?

▶ What would you definitely repeat?

▶ Did the children learn the skills that will help them get closer to your goal?

▶ What other knowledge or information might you need?

The process of reflection and self-evaluation used in the cycle of continuous improvement is as critical to your development as a teacher as a self-initiated activity is to a child's development.[2] Without evaluation, you won't be able to take the long view of what children are learning. Evaluation may lead you to try a completely different approach or varying approaches for different children in your care. You may have to review your goals to see if they are still relevant.

The Cycle of Continuous Improvement in Action

In the following examples, Pepe and Rachel use the cycle of continuous improvement to create a writing center and a loose parts center in their respective classrooms.

After a training on early literacy, Pepe decided he wanted to work on helping his children learn to write their names by the end of the year. One strategy he wanted to try was creating a writing center in his classroom. He found different sizes and colors of paper and many pencils, colored pencils, and crayons and placed them all at a table. He also put name cards, stencils, rulers, and erasers on the table. He knew children enjoyed writing notes and putting them in envelopes, so he included several sizes of envelopes. The first day, Pepe watched the writing center closely and asked himself these questions:

- Did children go to the writing center?
- What kinds of activities were they trying?
- How long were they staying?
- Did certain children avoid the center?

He noticed that the children went to the writing center but stayed only a short time. They put pieces of paper into the envelopes but didn't write on them. Two children didn't try anything at the writing center. Pepe knew these two children often avoided fine-motor activities.

Pepe decided to keep the writing center to give children a chance to explore it. But after reflecting on his observations, he also wanted to try giving the children more ideas about how to use the center. He introduced the writing center in his large group the next day. He showed the children the writing materials and discussed how to use them. By the next week, children were happily writing and copying the names on the name cards. In the third week, Pepe introduced a post office dramatic play theme that incorporated the writing center. Groups of children were now vying for seats at the writing center, and Pepe had to structure turns at the table.

He noticed that the same two children kept steering clear of the writing center. He observed these children more, and he wondered if they needed more fine-motor activities to strengthen their fingers. He put basters and measuring cups at the water table and encouraged the two children to play in the water and squeeze the basters to fill and empty them. Gradually, after a few weeks of fun activities with play dough, clay, water, and doll clothes with buttons, he helped the two children write with a pencil. He kept it short, and the children were willing to do it again the next day.

Pepe was confident he had found ways to engage all his children in the writing at the writing center, but he wasn't sure if they all were learning to write their names. After observing children's writing, he decided to add a sign-in activity when children entered the classroom. Children were able to sign in with help from their families. Pepe especially valued the involvement of families in this activity.

As Pepe established a writing center in his classroom, he was engaging in the cycle of continuous improvement—even though he might not call it that. He observed, both formally and informally, to see if he was meeting his goal of engaging children in the writing center. He had a long-term goal to accomplish, and he kept his eye on that as well. He altered and expanded his strategies and activities frequently, based on the responses of the children.

In the following example, Rachel also used the cycle of continuous improvement to carry out a new classroom strategy of loose parts. She was especially interested in using this strategy to engage children in early math. Rachel was committed to active, hands-on learning and was attracted to the idea of placing random, unconnected materials out on a table and asking children to play with them. Her story illustrates how a teacher makes a plan, tries it, evaluates it, and adapts it as needed.*

While perusing online groups for educators in child care settings (both in-home and center-based), Rachel began to notice many photographs and posts related to "loose parts." At first glance, loose parts are simply small piles of objects made accessible to the children in an early education setting. Often the loose parts are organized in some type of sectioned tray for sorting and easy access. The loose parts areas that Rachel read about were all left available for the children to use with little instruction or guidance. If children chose to explore the loose parts, however, a teacher could engage with them and help extend their learning by showing other interesting ways to use the loose parts. The idea to let the children discover the loose parts area and use it as they please is believed to increase creative thinking skills, and many educators noted that children often were seen sorting and counting the loose parts without instruction to do so. The loose parts concept sounded interesting to Rachel, but she wanted to take it a bit further into the mathematical world.

Rachel tried the loose parts in her own older preschool classroom full of four- and five-year-old children. She offered containers of small objects, ranging from the natural—acorns, twigs, shells, and so on—to colorful small toys made for classroom counting. Her classroom loose parts areas offered magnets, Legos, small transportation vehicles, Unifix Cubes, paper clips, small magnetic shapes, beads, gems, pom-poms, puzzle pieces, and more to explore. Each loose parts area also contained tools to enhance fine-motor development while engaging with the loose parts. Tools like tweezers,

---

* Adapted with permission of Rachel Pike.

magnetic wands, tongs, lacing string, pipe cleaners, and more offered many ways to move the loose parts from one container or area to another. Rachel knew that including measuring tools like scales and rulers, and dice for playing games with the loose parts, would invite children over to the loose parts area. She enhanced it with grid games, sorting trays, counting trays, ice cube trays (for creating patterns in or counting into), egg cartons with numerals written in each section, multicolored sorting bowls, tangram frames, puzzle frames, math word cards, and many other additions.

She learned right away, however, not to overdo it. At first, the preschoolers in Rachel's classroom responded to the loose parts area by dumping out all the cups of loose parts into a pile, then spending much of their free choice time cleaning up and resorting all the loose parts. The children and Rachel learned quickly that this left little time for other playing and learning. She tried the hands-off method that so many other child care providers had suggested. Unfortunately, using this method, her loose parts area just ended up being a mess. The mess prevented children from engaging in the materials, because most of their day was spent cleaning up the small items dumped everywhere.

Choosing a few different items rather than a huge variety, and keeping the number of each item under one hundred, seemed to work better. Also, Rachel suggested the children try taking only one or two kinds of loose parts out of the area at a time, then getting more if they wanted to, after exploring those items. This made sense to the children (especially the ones who had spent so much time cleaning up the objects). After rearranging the room, she gave a tour of the new toys in the room and said out loud different ways she might use the loose parts area. This approach planted ideas in the kids' heads and still allowed them to have independence in the area. Rachel also provided large-group introductions on how to play grid games and taught the games to a few children during free choice time. This led to them teaching other children and choosing to play grid games while exploring the loose parts on their own. Guiding and teaching ways to use the loose parts worked well in Rachel's classroom, but she always said, "This is one way we could use the loose parts area," so that no children felt limited in their creativity.

The older preschoolers were constantly choosing to sort items by color or type, making complicated patterns that sometimes used five different objects, lining up items, measuring objects in scales or with rulers and measuring tape, and counting in the loose parts area. Children played math games in the loose parts area during free choice time, and they chose the area as a popular station during small-group activity times. Throughout free choice time, Rachel observed the math skills of sorting, graphing, measuring, counting, addition, subtraction, and patterning integrated into much of the preschoolers' dramatic play. Math became a daily constant in her classroom, and she couldn't have been happier. Since implementing the loose parts area in her classroom, Rachel has seen a statistically significant increase in her preschoolers' abilities to recognize, copy, extend, and create patterns and to count objects one-to-one.

Rachel observed, "The addition of a loose parts area to our classroom has improved the mathematical skills of all our preschoolers and has helped staff feel more comfortable engaging in math with the children. Preschoolers are able to explore the loose parts with creative and imaginative thinking. Teachers also provide many ideas and guidance for using the loose parts in ways that advance their mathematical skills. At first glance, loose parts are simply small piles of objects made accessible to the children in an early education setting. At second glance, the loose parts area is oh so much more."[3]

As we read Rachel's story, we see many examples of thoughtful, mindful teaching. First, she found an idea that matched with her teaching philosophy, her curriculum, and her children's interests. She was curious about how this idea would work with her children. Although she set it up to connect to early math, she wasn't really sure how that would play out.

Second, Rachel formed a plan to provide children with loose parts on a tray. Then she carried out her plan. She watched the children carefully as they encountered the new materials.

Third, Rachel decided the children's prolonged explorations of loose parts involved more cleanup than learning. As she evaluated the activity, she formed ideas about how she could make it more effective, especially for math learning.

Fourth, Rachel made changes in the activity. She pulled back some of the materials and limited the number of each type of item to one hundred. She guided the children and gave suggestions about how to use the materials. At large-group time, she discussed grid games and how the loose parts could be used.

At the end of her story, Rachel saw the children using the loose parts for early math learning. They were engaged, interested, and growing in their ability to explore the materials to form and answer their own questions. Rachel knew the loose parts activity would keep changing as her group's or her own interests changed. But she also knew that the knowledge she gained from this exploration would help her as she designed new strategies.

Hopes, Fears, and Burning Questions

Chapter 4 discussed an activity we did with teachers as we started our work with them. We asked teachers to write down their hopes for their students and themselves, their worries and fears, and any burning questions they wanted answered.

At the end of our project, we revisited the teachers' hopes, fears, and burning questions. Many were surprised at how their attitudes had changed.

In the beginning, many teachers had been worried about having enough time to make instructional changes. By the end of the project, the teachers found that they did have enough time; they just learned to use their time differently. For instance, teachers were committed to keeping their large groups short—fifteen to twenty minutes—and were worried about adding another math activity into the large-group time. They found they could still keep the group times short and engaging by adding a small math component to their read-alouds.

At the beginning of our project, some teachers had been concerned that their children couldn't do the work we proposed, and the teachers were hesitant to push the children. By the end of the project, the teachers no longer felt this way. They were surprised at how much young children loved learning math and literacy. Because the teachers did careful evaluation, they knew when a child felt pushed, and therefore when they should back off for a while. But more often, teachers were delighted at how much children could do and how much they enjoyed the challenge.

When you read Chapter 4, you filled out the reproducible form "Hopes, Fears, and Burning Questions," (pages 85–86). Look at that worksheet again. Have your hopes, fears, and burning questions changed? What do you hope as you continue your journey to intentionality? What are your fears? What are your questions? Although you are finishing this book now, your journey will go on. You will continue to grow as a teacher. Fill out this form again whenever you are facing changes in your teaching practice.

> Your efforts at becoming an effective teacher benefit the children you teach and enrich your life.

Being an intentional teacher keeps you interested in teaching and learning, and it provides many opportunities for growth. Your observations of children and how to engage them shows you ways to be creative and open to change. Your efforts at becoming an effective teacher benefit the children you teach and enrich your life. As educator Peter Gow points out in his book *The Intentional Teacher*, "For our intentional teacher, it will be the students whose lives have been touched in the course of that career that will indeed form the core of lasting memories of a life well and purposefully lived."[4]

We, too, have hopes for you as you continue your journey. Teaching young children and influencing their lives is some of the most fulfilling work we have done. We hope you will find it as satisfying as we have. May your journey be filled with enthusiastic children, engaged families, interesting colleagues, and many opportunities for you to grow, learn, and improve your skills. May any problems you encounter be small and easy to solve. And may you remember how what you believe and value guides your work. Enjoy the ride!

References

1. Jeanne Dickhausen, "Jeanne's Journey" (unpublished manuscript, September 12, 2014).

2. Alma Fleet and Catherine Patterson, "Professional Growth Reconceptualized: Early Childhood Staff Searching for Meaning," *Early Childhood Research and Practice* 3, no. 2 (Fall 2001), ecrp.uiuc.edu/v2n2/fleet.html.

3. Rachel Pike, "Rachel's Story" (unpublished manuscript, September 12, 2014).

4. Peter Gow, *The Intentional Teacher* (Gilsum, NH: Avocus Publishing, 2009): 184.

My Journey

How have you changed as a teacher?

What has changed since you
began teaching?

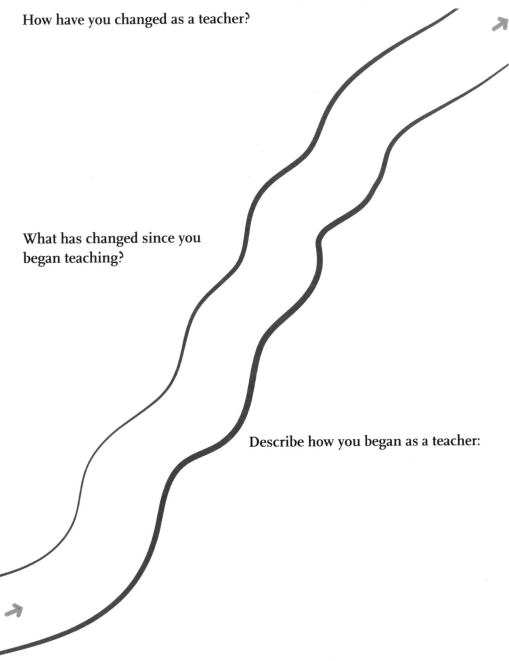

Describe how you began as a teacher:

BIBLIOGRAPHY

Beijaard, Douwe, Paulien C. Meijer, and Nico Verloop. "Reconsidering Research on Teachers' Professional Identity." *Teaching and Teacher Education* 20 (2004): 107–128.

Borton, Terry. *Reach, Touch, and Teach: Student Concerns and Process Education.* New York: McGraw-Hill, 1970.

Cain, Susan. *Quiet: The Power of Introverts in a World That Can't Stop Talking.* New York: Crown Publishing Group, 2013.

Connelly, F. Michael, and D. Jean Clandinin. "Personal Practical Knowledge and the Modes of Knowing: Relevance for Teaching and Learning." In *Learning and Teaching the Ways of Knowing*, edited by Elliot Eisner, 174–198. Chicago: University of Chicago Press, 1985.

Connelly, F. Michael, and D. Jean Clandinin. *Shaping a Professional Identity.* New York: Teachers College Press, 1999.

Derman-Sparks, Louise, and Julie Olsen Edwards. *Anti-Bias Education for Young Children and Ourselves.* Washington, DC: NAEYC, 2010.

Dickhausen, Jeanne. "Jeanne's Journey." Unpublished manuscript, last modified September 12, 2014.

Dobson, Gwen. "Gwen's Story." Unpublished manuscript, last modified September 19, 2014.

Dreyfus, Hubert L., and Stuart E. Dreyfus. *Mind Over Machine: The Power of Human Intuition and Expertise in the Era of the Computer.* New York: Free Press, 1986, quoted in Dall'Alba, Gloria, and Jörgen Sandberg, "Unveiling Professional Development: A Critical Review of Stage Models," *Review of Educational Research* 76, no. 3 (2006): 383–412.

Dweck, Carol S. *Mindset: The New Psychology of Success.* New York: Random House, 2006.

Epstein, Ann S. *The Intentional Teacher: Choosing the Best Strategies for Young Children's Learning.* Washington, DC: NAEYC, 2014.

Fleet, Alma, and Catherine Patterson. "Professional Growth Reconceptualized: Early Childhood Staff Searching for Meaning." *Early Childhood Research and Practice* 3, no. 2 (Fall 2001). ecrp.uiuc.edu/v2n2/fleet.html.

Forman, George. "Mirrors That Talk: Using Video to Improve Early Education." *Connections* (January 2002): 1. eclkc.ohs.acf.hhs.gov/hslc/tta-system/teaching /eecd/domains%20of%20child%20development/science/mirrors.pdf.

Ginsburg, Herbert P., Rochelle Goldberg Kaplan, Joanna Cannon, Maria I. Cordero, Janet G. Eisenband, Michelle Galanter, and Melissa Morgenlander. "Helping Early Childhood Educators Teach Mathematics." In *Critical Issues in Early Childhood Professional Development,* edited by Martha Zaslow and Ivelisse Martinez-Beck, 171–202. Baltimore: Paul H. Brookes Publishing Company, 2006.

Gow, Peter. *The Intentional Teacher.* Gilsum, NH: Avocus Publishing, 2009.

Guinan, Sylvia. "Why Do Teachers Teach?" August 15, 2013. www.wiziq.com/teachblog/why-do-teachers-teach.

Harada, Violet H., Debora Lum, and Kathy Souza. "Building a Learning Community: Students and Adults as Inquirers." *Childhood Education* (Winter 2002–2003): 68–71.

Harrison, Cindy, and Joellen Killion. "Ten Roles for Teacher Leaders." *Educational Leadership* 65, no. 1 (2007): 74–77.

Heidemann, Sandra, and Deborah Hewitt. *When Play Isn't Fun: Helping Children Resolve Play Conflicts.* Saint Paul, MN: Redleaf Press, 2014.

Helm, Judy Harris. "Building Communities of Practice." *Young Children* 62, no. 4 (2007): 12–16.

Jerve, Janet. "Janet's Story." Unpublished manuscript, last modified September 19, 2014.

Katz, Lilian G. "Developmental Stages of Preschool Teachers." *Elementary School Journal* 73, no. 1 (1972): 50–54.

Kaufman, Alan. *Our Identities: Multicultural Readings for Writers.* Dubuque, IA: Kendall/Hunt Publishing Company, 1994.

Landry, Susan H., Jason L. Anthony, Paul R. Swank, and Pauline Monseque-Bailey. "Effectiveness of Comprehensive Professional Development for Teachers of At-Risk Preschoolers." *Journal of Educational Psychology* 101, no. 2 (2009): 448–465.

LaParo, Karen M., Robert C. Pianta, and Megan Stuhlman."The Classroom Assessment Scoring System: Findings from the Prekindergarten Year." *The Elementary School Journal* 104, no. 5 (2004): 409–426.

Longfield, Judith. "Discrepant Teaching Events: Using an Inquiry Stance to Address Student's Misconceptions." *International Journal of Teaching and Learning in Higher Education* 21, no. 2 (2009): 266–271.

Mackenzie, Sarah V., and George Marnik. "Maine Program Helps Teachers Learn from That Voice: Inner Voice Tells Teachers How to Grow." *Journal of Staff Development* 25, no. 3 (Summer 2004): 50–57.

Marsick, Victoria J., and Karen E. Watkins. "Continuous Learning in the Workplace." *Adult Learning* 3, no. 4 (1992): 9–12.

Mowry, Brian. "Engaging and Developing Young Children's Informal Number Sense." Presentation at the Numbers Work! Institute, Saint Paul, MN, March 8, 2013.

NAEYC. "Developmentally Appropriate Practice." NAEYC, 2009. www.naeyc.org/DAP.

NAEYC. "Screening and Assessment of Young English-Language Learners." NAEYC, 2005. www.naeyc.org/files/naeyc/file/positions/ELL_Supplement Long.pdf.

National Education Goals Panel. *Principles and Recommendations for Early Childhood Assessments.* Washington, DC: U.S. Government Printing Office, 1998.

Nicholson, Simon. "The Theory of Loose Parts: An Important Principle for Design Methodology." *Studies in Design Education Craft and Technology* 4, no. 2 (1972): 5–14.

Piaget, Jean. *Biology and Knowledge.* Chicago: University of Chicago Press, 1971.

Pianta, Robert C. "Standardized Observation and Professional Development: A Focus on Individualized Implementation and Practice." In *Critical Issues in Early Childhood Professional Development*, edited by Martha Zaslow and Ivelisse Martinez-Beck, 231–254. Baltimore: Paul H. Brookes Publishing Company, 2006.

Pike, Rachel. "Rachel's Story." Unpublished manuscript, last modified September 12, 2014.

Riley, David, and Mary A. Roach. "Helping Teachers Grow: Toward Theory and Practice of an 'Emergent Curriculum' Model of Staff Development." *Early Childhood Education Journal* 33, no. 5 (2006): 363–370.

Rogoff, Barbara. *Developing Destinies: A Mayan Midwife and Town*. New York: Oxford University Press, 2011.

Rowe, D. W. "Examining Teacher Talk: Revealing Hidden Boundaries for Curricular Change." *Language Arts* 75, no. 2 (1998): 103–107.

Sandberg, Jörgen, and Gloria Dall'Alba. "Returning to Practice Anew: A Life-World Perspective." *Organization Studies* 30, no. 12 (2009): 1349–1368.

Sheridan, Susan M., Carolyn Pope Edwards, Christin A. Marvin, and Lisa L. Knoche. "Professional Development in Early Childhood Classrooms: Process Issues and Research Needs." *Early Education and Development* 20, no. 3 (2009): 377–401.

Snow-Renner, Ravay, and Patricia A. Lauer. *McRel Insights: Professional Development Analysis*. Denver: McRel, 2005.

Wenger, Etienne R. *Communities of Practice: Learning, Meaning, and Identity*. New York: Cambridge University Press, 1998, quoted in Helm, Judy Harris, "Building Communities of Practice," *Young Children* 62, no. 4 (2007): 12–16.

Whitehead, Catherine. "Definition of Learning Style." eHow. Accessed September 17, 2015. www.ehow.com/about_6551473_definition-learning-style.html.

INDEX

ABOUT THE AUTHORS

Sandra Heidemann, M.S., is a decades-long veteran of early childhood education who has been dedicated to helping all children feel included and valued. During her career, she has been a teacher, infant home visitor, director, trainer, author, and past board president of the Minnesota Association for the Education of Young Children (MnAEYC). She currently serves on the board of Southside Family Nurturing Center. Sandra has published articles in the journal *Young Children* and the magazine *Exchange* and is the coauthor of the book *Play: The Pathway from Theory to Practice* and two related workbooks, *When Play Isn't Fun* and *When Play Isn't Easy*, published by Redleaf Press.

Beth Menninga, M.A.Ed., is inspired by the dedication and creativity of early childhood practitioners. As project coordinator for the Center for Early Education and Development at the University of Minnesota, she focuses her work on design and delivery of training, promotion of coaching, and reflective practice in infant and toddler development, early mathematics, and literacy. Her own journey began as a child care teacher. She has coordinated professional development initiatives on infant and toddler caregiving, early literacy, and math. Beth sees her work with young children, families, and early childhood educators as a commitment to social justice. She lives in Minneapolis with her husband, daughter, and dog.

Claire Chang, M.A., has worked to increase family stability and vitality through services benefiting parents and children by improving child outcomes through high-quality early childhood programs. She has served on the governing board of the National Association for the Education of Young Children (NAEYC) and chaired the Accreditation Council. Recognized as a leader in her community on issues of equity and access, Claire serves on the board of Hope Community and Luther Seminary. Claire has a B.S. in child development and family life from the University of Wisconsin–Stout and an M.A. in philanthropy and development from Saint Mary's University of Winona, Minnesota.

More Great Books from Free Spirit

A Moving Child Is a Learning Child
How the Body Teaches the Brain to Think (Birth to Age 7)
by Gill Connell
and Cheryl McCarthy
*336 pp., full color, PB, 7¼" x 9¼".
Teachers, caregivers, special education practitioners, clinicians, and parents of children ages 0–7.*

Move, Play, and Learn with Smart Steps
Sequenced Activities to Build the Body and the Brain (Birth to Age 7)
by Gill Connell, Wendy Pirie, M.H.Sc., and Cheryl McCarthy
*216 pp., full color, PB, 8½" x 11".
Early childhood teachers, caregivers, program directors, coaches, mentors, professional development trainers, and parents (of children birth to age 7).
Includes digital content.*

Teaching Gifted Children in Today's Preschool and Primary Classrooms
Identifying, Nurturing, and Challenging Children Ages 4–9
by Joan Franklin Smutny, M.A.,
Sally Yahnke Walker, Ph.D.,
and Ellen I. Honeck, Ph.D.
*248 pp., PB, 8½" x 11".
Educators, grades preK–3.
Includes digital content.*

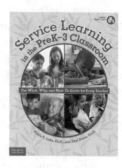

Service Learning in the PreK–3 Classroom
The What, Why, and How-To Guide for Every Teacher
by Vickie E. Lake, Ph.D.
and Ithel Jones, Ed.D.
*224 pp., PB, 8½" x 11".
Educators, administrators, and early childhood professionals, grades preK–3.
Includes digital content.*

Activities for Building Character and Social-Emotional Learning PreK–K
Safe & Caring Schools® Series
by Katia S. Petersen, Ph.D.
*160 pp., PB, 8½" x 11".
Educators, group leaders, caregivers, grades preK–K.
Includes digital content.*

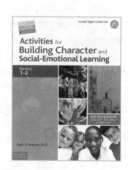

Activities for Building Character and Social-Emotional Learning Grades 1–2
Safe & Caring Schools® Series
by Katia S. Petersen, Ph.D.
*208 pp., PB, 8½" x 11".
Educators, group leaders, caregivers, grades 1–2.
Includes digital content.*

Interested in purchasing multiple quantities and receiving volume discounts?
Contact edsales@freespirit.com or call 1.800.735.7323 and ask for Education Sales.

Many Free Spirit authors are available for speaking engagements, workshops, and keynotes.
Contact speakers@freespirit.com or call 1.800.735.7323.

For pricing information, to place an order, or to request a free catalog, contact:

**Free Spirit Publishing Inc. • 6325 Sandburg Road, Suite 100 • Minneapolis, MN 55427-3674
toll-free 800.735.7323 • local 612.338.2068 • fax 612.337.5050
help4kids@freespirit.com • www.freespirit.com**